Other family history books by Trevor N Price

MORGAN PRICE & family … Wales & Southland, NZ.
The THOMAS family … (John & Uncle George) Devon, England & NZ.
WILLIAM THOMAS & family … Devon, England & NZ.
The STEVENS family … Devon, England & Canterbury, NZ.
Winner of The Keven McNulty Award, NZ Society of Genealogists
The WOODS family … Wales; Norfolk, England; NZ Wellington & Auckland.

NELSON PRICE

Pte 471269

WORLD WAR 2 DIARY

First published 2021 by:
Starting Gun Books, Auckland, New Zealand

National Library of New Zealand Cataloguing-in-Publication Data

Price, Trevor N. (Trevor Nelson), 1937-
NELSON PRICE (Pte 471269): World War 2 Diary / T.N. Price.
Includes bibliographical references and index.

ISBN 978-0-473-60084-6

Cover by Xanthe Price
Printed by Lightning Source

Nelson's Diary
Measures 105 X 150 mm

Nelson's Dog Tags ...
2 plastic discs strung on a boot lace. Both discs have "NZ 471269" stamped on them. These were always around his neck for identification.

Nelson while in Burnham Camp, New Zealand 1942

AUTHOR'S NOTE:

We have typed **NELSON'S WW2 DIARY** **full width of each page**.

Indented sections are extracts from WW2 historical documents, books, telegrams, etc, as detailed in Acknowledgments page 119, or are my comments signed (T).

The Diary is provided as written by Nelson, in his own words and in his own abbreviations and descriptions (refer page 114).

All troops used similar nick-names and slang words at that time.
New Zealanders were no different to troops from other countries and no real disrespect was meant to any person or country.

Nelson did not know we were going to print his war notes and thoughts, when he was jotting them down.

He probably referred to his dairy when he wrote home to keep them all advised and involved in his war activity.

Those who received his correspondence were ....
Lin / Lillian .. his wife.
Mrs J Price = Hannah Price / Mum .. his mother.
Mrs P W Thomas .. Lillian's mother Elsie.
Mrs Rose-Smith ... Jessie nee Stevens .. Elsie's sister
Jessie Hockings ...Lillian's life-long best friend Jessie
Mrs Hockings .. Daisy nee Stevens and Jessie's mother
F J Price .. Nelson's brother Frank
D Price .. Nelson's brother Dave
Harold .. Nelson's brother H.E.A. Price
Mrs Holloway .. Nelson's friend Charley / Chas' wife Olive.
Vera .. Nelson's sister, married to Wilson Blakie.

CONTENTS:

NEW ZEALAND

1942 … On June 18, Nelson Price filled in a form headed….

NEW ZEALAND MILITARY FORCES
ATTESTATION FOR SERVICE IN TIME OF WAR,
WITHIN AND BEYOND NEW ZEALAND

This form contained his birth date … 6 December 1910, that he lived at 77 Wilton St, Invercargill, was married to Lillian Elsie Price, had 2 children, and was aged 31 years 6 months. His last occupation was with the Southland Times Company, as a Service Car Driver.

He signed the enlistment papers and was given
the NZ Army number … 471269

… On 16 July Nelson was required to make a Will…
which he did with solicitors W G & J Tait, Esk St, Invercargill.

… On 21 July Nelson entered camp, as part of 6th Canterbury Regiment and was assigned a bed in B Block, Burnham Camp, situated south and near to Christchurch City.

Nelson marching at Burnham Camp in 1942

Nelson on a motor bike, with Charlie (Chas) Holloway, at Burnham Camp, NZ, in 1942.

Another photo of <u>Nelson at Burnham Camp, NZ</u> on yet another motorbike.

Other parts of the NZ Army were in Egypt fighting the Germans at El Alamein, from July to November 1942, when Nelson was still in New Zealand.

He joined up in June 1942. He must have heard or read about the Despatch Riders racing around the sand hills on motor-bikes, dodging bullets, and delivering messages …

between NZ Army officials. He must have talked about it a lot and probably wished he could get into that part of the Army. Didn't happen though.

He was always happy moving on wheels and he would have enjoyed the journey from Waianawa to Waikiwi pre marriage, also driving the Rural Delivery Car and driving Tuffrey's buses.

1942 On November 5 Nelson was transferred from 6th Canterbury to the 1st Otago Regiment and soon travelled to train at the NZ Army Camp at Waiwera South.
(This was half way between Clinton and Balclutha. T)

--o0o—

1943

... Over the following seven months Nelson seems to have been given three 'home leaves' for a few days, until 26 June 1943 when *'Private Nelson Price marched in for overseas service'* as part of the 1st Otago Regiment.

... His regiment and a number of others, soon became the ....
"New Zealand 10th Reinforcements".

... 23 July 1943, Nelson embarked on a ship for EGYPT
and on this date his own Diary starts .. pages 12 to 119.

--o0o—

Before Nelson went overseas the Church gave him a small bible which had the following typed, inside the cover.

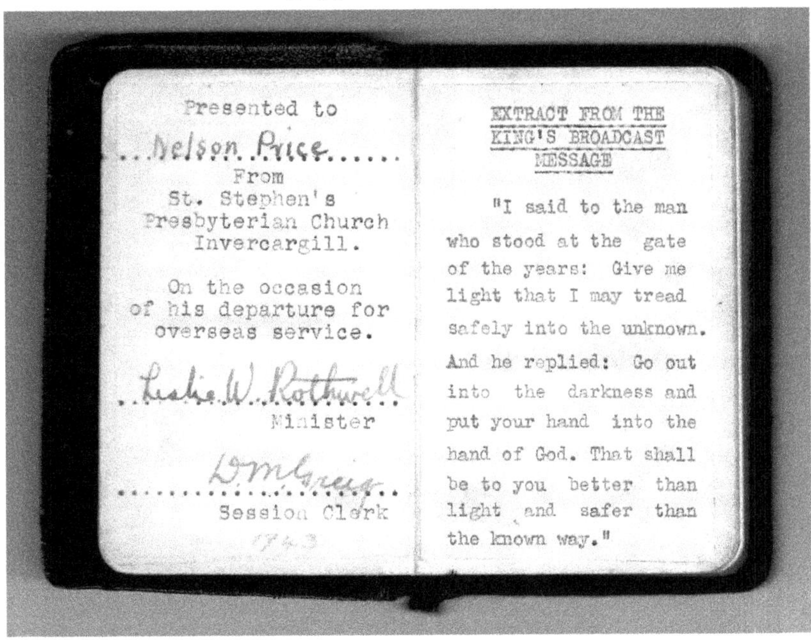

Presented to
Nelson Price
From
St. Stephen's
Presbyterian Church
Invercargill.

On the occasion
of his departure for
overseas service.

Leslie W. Rothwell
Minister

D M Greig
Session Clerk

EXTRACT FROM THE
KING'S BROADCAST
MESSAGE

"I said to the man who stood at the gate of the years: Give me light that I may tread safely into the unknown. And he replied: Go out into the darkness and put your hand into the hand of God. That shall be to you better than light and safer than the known way."

At the rear of this Bible his mother and his wife wrote ....

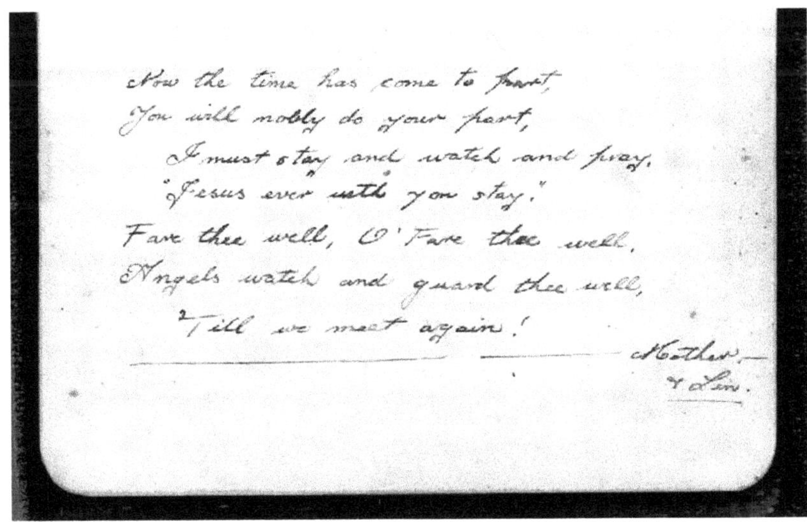

Now the time has come to part,
You will nobly do your part,
I must stay and watch and pray,
"Jesus ever with you stay."
Fare thee well, O' Fare thee well,
Angels watch and guard thee well,
'Till we meet again!

Mother —
& Len.

WORLD WAR 2 ...
DIARY of NELSON PRICE

Private Nelson Price #471269
3 Section, 11 Platoon,
B Company, 26 Battalion,
2.N.Z.E.F.

Home address ...
77 Wilton St,
North Invercargill,
Southland,
New Zealand.

Bren #2358, Rifle #94783
#1 on Bren Gun, Dave H Parr #92408
Wyndham, Southland, NZ
(Nelson was #2 on the Bren Gun team.)

WORLD WAR 2, 23 July 1943
Nelson on this date was aged 32.5, married, with two children.

NEW ZEALAND 1943:

23rd July... Friday. Cabin 213, A Deck.
Left Wellington at 6am. Was down below in the mess-room doing my job as Orderly. Didn't see the actual leaving of the wharf, but got up on deck later and watched the hills of Wellington disappear, with a feeling of despair and not a little tightening of throat muscles. Thought of Lin (wife Lillian) and kiddies, hated to leave them to battle along on their own, but I wasn't boss, so couldn't do much about it. Felt a bit squirmy as the *"Amsterdam"* tossed up and down. Amsterdam big liner 38,000 tons. Made all other boats look small. Accommodation pretty packed. About six thousand men on board.

The *"SS NIEUW AMSTERDAM"* was requisitioned by the British Ministry of Transport from the Dutch. After the tourist interior was removed, she was converted to troop use, with three hammocks high in the sleeping areas. The exterior was painted grey and in six years she carried 378631 men to WW2. (T)

AUSTRALIA 1943:

27th July... Made Hobart about 2.30pm on Thursday 27th. Nice day. Weren't allowed ashore but stood on deck and saw real Aussies for first time. Looked just like Kiwis except for brim of hat turned up. Took on board about 50 prisoners of war. Some from the Islands. One was a girl, German spy, very pretty with long brunette hair. Most of the prisoners were old and of mixed sexes. Some in German Luftwaffe uniform. Looked very trim and proud. Some were merchant ship's captains and some hard to say what they were.

We stayed in port 4 hours, took on water and potatoes etc, and left about 6.30pm enroute for Perth. Previous crossing of Tasman was very rough. Crew said it was roughest sea they had ever been on and they had been at sea for 4 years on war work. Good chaps and pure bred Dutchmen. Very patriotic and obliging.

2nd August... After a trip of 6 days we arrived at Perth in Western Australia. Had to stand outside harbour for hours awaiting pilot boat. Got ashore at 2pm for leave to Perth. Harbour was Fremantle and about 11 miles from Perth. Had to go by train to Perth. Wonderful place. Nice town but narrow streets. Got Lin & kiddies a card each and cable sent. Felt better for it. Chas Holloway, Doug, Lou, Michael, Arch Court and I all kept together. Went to pictures at night. Got back to boat about 12.30pm and was given cup of coffee and biscuit by YMCA mobile canteen. Was good and very much appreciated.

3rd August... Lin's birthday. Good old kid. Wished I was with her to celebrate it instead of where I was. Went on leave again with Chas, Ernie Brown and Doug. Went to Zoo and enjoyed it except for headache and `land legs'. Had big feed at Perth. Made up for so much custard on boat. Got back to boat about 12 midnight.

4th August... Boat sailed 6am for across the Indian Ocean. Very calm sea all the way. Hardly a ripple. Became hotter as we approached the Equator. Slept out on deck every night. Lay awake at night thinking of every throb of engine putting distance between Lin and kiddies and I. Pretty tough.

9th August... Crossed Equator at 6 am. Two guns fired as signal. A German prisoner died… was buried at sea.

10th to 17th August… Nothing recorded. (Was travelling at sea. T)

--o0o--

EGYPT 1943:

18th August... Arrived at Port Tufix, Egypt, near the Suez Canal about 8am. (Port Tawfiq or Port Tewfik on maps) Very hot. 14 days from Perth. Awaited disembarking orders until about 2pm. Chas went off in first scow enroute to Maadi. Boarded the lighter and taken ashore at Tufix.

'Amsterdam' looked big all by herself in harbour.

Got feet on land again. Heat was sweltering. Hardly breathe. Had cup of tea and a couple of pies, all free from the YMCA Tent.
Very much appreciated.
Acres of trucks awaiting us. Drivers looked very brown and tough. Us new hands all pale legged and pale face and hands. Big contrast. Got on trucks. Twenty with gear to truck. Driver gave us two tins water which was to drink. Was hot nearly couldn't drink it but later on had to.

Set off for Cairo and our camp. Road very dusty till we got on bitumen. Arrived Cairo about 9pm. Just getting dark. All eyes and ears. Pretty stinking place, fine buildings, funny people, funny carts. (see photo page 16) Got to Mena base camp, 11 miles from Cairo past Pyramids at dark. Slept in tents. (see photo page 17)

Was at Mena a fortnight and had two leaves into Cairo from there.

(Nelson does not mention The Sphinx but this photo is in his War Photo Album. T.)

STREET SCENE IN CAIRO. Bit different to our NZ city look. Did Nelson carry a camera throughout his war travels ? (T)

Was shifted to Maadi where I joined the 2NZEF. Was put in ... Infantry Co, 3 Section, 11 Platoon, B Company, 26 Battalion. NZ. Good crowd of chaps. Not many old hands left.

(Maadi Camp was in the Gindali region of Egypt, mid-way between Cairo and Suez and offered some experience of hills but none of mud, hard going and thick vegetation.) (I)

--o0o--

The men of the **"New Zealand Expeditionary Forces 10th Reinforcements"** paraded for General Bernard Freyberg at Mena Camp, Egypt, on 22 August 1943. (Nat Lib NZ)

(Nelson is one of those fellows marching on parade.)

NZ CAMP MENA, EGYPT.... As at **30 August 1943.**
(ex Nat Lib NZ)

30 August... Lillian received a Telegram from NZ Minister of Defence Mr F Jones ... "Nelson reached his destination safely."

A POSTCARD made in Cairo and sent to Lillian in New Zealand.
..... Lillian 30, Trevor 5, and Marlene 3.5 years. (T)

This photo was taken of Nelson early **in Egypt 1943**, and we believe used in the composite photo of himself, Lillian and their two children, with the Nile and pyramids on page 17.(T)

A photo of Nelson ...
... "ON GUARD" ...

Sorry, we have no idea where this was taken. Could have been at Burnham, NZ or in Egypt, or in Italy. (T)

Nelson sent this Egyptian hand-worked velvet wall hanging home.

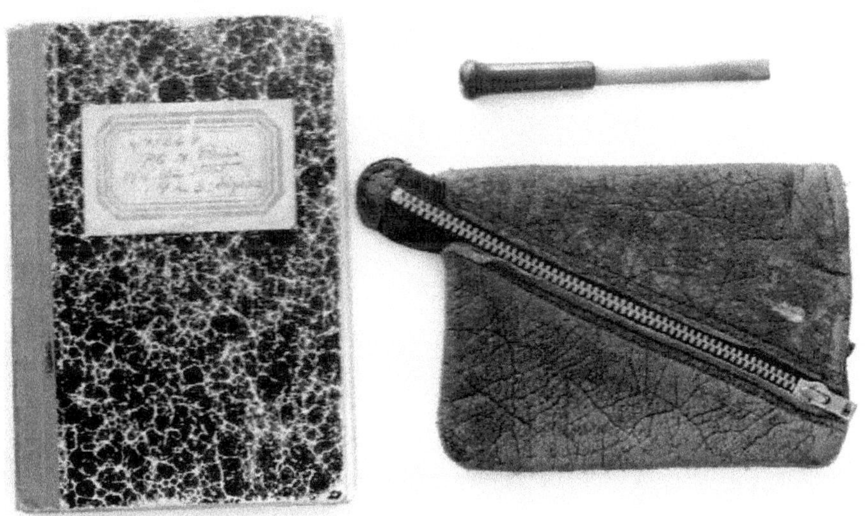

Nelson's Diary, and his cigarette holder and tobacco pouch.
A habit he gave up soon after returning to New Zealand.

THE TIMES ROLL OF HONOUR

Members of Staff in Armed Forces as at 1st September, 1943.

LITERARY DEPARTMENT

Lt. R. S. Brown (killed in action)
P/O. R. G. Lund
Capt. S. G. Dinniss
2nd/Lt. A. J. Goldfinch
Sgt. L. F. Hannon (wounded)
S./Sgt. N. E. Pierce
Pte. A. A. Brown
A.C.2 I. D. MacGregor
O. Sig. D. Stone
Sig. T. B. McNee (on leave)
L.A.C. J. R. Redpath
O.S. J. T. Bridgman
Sgt. C. J. (Mrs) Webb, nee Gilmour

LINOTYPE OPERATORS

Flying-Officer A. D. D. Jackson
2nd/Lt. L. H. Wills (returned from Middle East).
W.O.2 A. W. H. McKenzie
2nd/Lt. J. T. Wilson
Sig. M. Rattray
Pte. D. M. Beck (prisoner of war)
Pte. T. R. Stewart (prisoner of war)
Pte. J. E. Lawry

COMPOSING ROOM, JOBBING, STEREO, ROTARY PRESS

Lt. G. McAnergney
Sgt-Pilot K. Shaw
Cpl. C. G. Couling (on leave)
A.C.2 E. H. Winter
L./Cpl. J. W. Reed
Cpl. J. Gillespie
Pte. A. S. Grant (prisoner of war, now repatriated)
Sgt. G. V. Shirley, M.M. (1918)
Pte. C. H. Parks, M.M.
Pte. W. Mitchell

MAIL CAR DRIVERS

Sgt. H. W. Rogers
A.C.1. D. A. Anderson
Gnr. L. A. Shaw
Pte. N. Price
Pte. C. E. Holloway
A.C.2 A. N. McEwan

COMMERCIAL OFFICE

L.A.C. G. Kilpatrick
Pte. J. R. O'Brien
A.C.1 F. N. Anderson

Nelson (5 lines up) was an employee of The Southland Times before the War … his friend Chas Holloway was also a Mail Car Diver.

6th September... Went out on manoeuvres into the desert, 6th Brigade show. Went about 20 mile to a fairly flat place where we camped for the night in bivvies. (bivouac shelter ... 1 or 2 man tent) Had to have a picket on, on account of wandering Arabs. Pinch anything but mostly rifles if they get a chance. Always sleep with rifle in bed with me. Not near so nice and comforting as dear old Lin, but under circumstances quite a good pal to have. Jim Wakefield was bivvy companion during manoeuvre.

7th September ... Packed up and travelled about 20 mile and dug in, in defensive positions. Met Dan McDonald a pipper. Had long yarn.

8th September... Slept beside slit trenches and `stood to' at 5.30am.
Broke camp at 6am and went to see a demonstration shoot from a hilltop by 25 pounders, mortars and machine guns. Looked real & pretty deadly. Big bangs and smoke bombs.

<u>Nelson at The Red Sea area</u> trying to hide the bandage on his right leg, mentioned on 9th September.

9th September... Went another 20 mile and camped for night. Nothing of importance happening.
26th Battalion went ahead to act as ambushing party in big defile. Climbed up on top of hills and over-looked convoy going through. Chas rode through on bike and fell off but I didn't see him.

Arrived at Red Sea about 3 pm and had a swim. Skinned my leg on a rock and got it dressed at R.A.P. Was pretty sore. (see page 21)

10th September... Broke camp and returned to Maadi about 12 noon. Had a shower and felt much better.

11th September... Went to pictures a few times while in Maadi.

The Battalion transport ready to leave Maadi, September 1943

15th September... Left Maadi by trucks (photo above) on 105 mile route-march to Alexandria. Didn't fancy the idea much, thought of poor old feet, blisters etc. Arrived at Mena first night, the starting point, and got underway at 6pm. Marched 50 minutes, then 10 minute spells. Trucks went ahead and made camp about 14 miles away. Got there about 11pm. Had a cup of tea and sandwich and crawled into bed. Very tired.

(First stage of the move was the transfer of the Division to Burg el Arab on the coast. The convoy stopped and all ranks debussed to continue the journey on foot. The march was to extend over seven days, the troops resting during the heat of the day and beginning their march at sunset. Ambulances would follow to pick up those with blistered feet. After treatment these men would be graded A, B or C and only grade C were given a ride for the rest of the way. On the first two nights RAP attended over 80 men. By the time the march ended few men were without blisters.) (O)

(The Division made the longest march on foot in its history, the most gruelling of a series of exertions planned to harden the troops for the rigours of an Italian winter.) (I)

16th September... Today went to R.A.P. with poisoned leg. Doctor said "You ride in truck tonight. Boot make it worse." Was very pleased but did not let on. Did the truck ride for three nights and erected platoon bivvies when I got there. Don't know which was the hardest. Marching or erecting bivvies. 5th night I was on the march again, leg better ... `worst luck'. Marched in sandals that night. Next two nights in boots.

20th September... Passed through Amiriya, first place since leaving Mena, all the rest desert. Just sand, sand and more sand. Trucks waiting at junction of 'Alexandria' and `Bir el Arab' roads for us. Got on and went three hours to camping place at Bir el Arab, about 300 yards from shore of Mediterranean. Was dark when we arrived at 2am. (Birg el Arab area is west of Alexandria, Egypt. T)

21st September... Awoke to the music of the cookhouse stove. Had a look around our new temporary home. Saw date palms and fig trees. Some chaps had some figs and later were told off by Major Smith. Figs were the property of the Wogs and we had to leave them

alone. We used to wait until dark and then raid them. I liked figs in the raw state fine.
Rested up all day and gave blisters and scalded feet a chance to heal up. Swam with Bob Henderson in the Med and scrounged along the beach for shells or crabs or bits of sponge.

22nd & 23rd September... Nothing recorded.

24th September... Went out on a firing and movement course, assaulted a sand hill, picking figs as we went in the attack and finished up firing everything we had into the sea, at birds or at tins.

I fired for the first time out of **A BREN GUN** and shot up tins from the hip and showering sand everywhere. I like the old bren gun fire but sand didn't improve the mechanism much.

25th September... Left today on a four day Brigade manoeuvre. Arrived about 11pm, miles into the desert, picked our bivvy spot and slept heartily. Dog tired.

26th September... Lay doggo for all day and the next, reading. Wrote a letter to Lin and one to Mum. At night was to come the big barrage, the final stunt. At 8pm we had ourselves inside our respirators, web, small pack, ground sheet, water bottle, rifle, and a shovel poked down inside our air web. We looked like pack horses. Was just at our first stop (spell) when I spotted Chas in the gloom. Yelled out `Holloway, you old so and so' and he came over and had a good laugh at the said pack-horse. We marched for two hours on to our start line, a white tape put down to tell us how far the enemy was away. Had to wait three hours until zero hour ... 2 am, when

the attack was launched. At 2am sharp we got the order to advance and at the same time overcame the barrage. What a hell of a din and the yellowish blue light attached to the explosions and artillery fire was blinding. For two minutes I felt squirmy and wished I was 1 foot tall and 2 inches thick. Shells, (25 pounders) screamed overhead with a zzzrrrrrr & when landing ... whoooofffff.
One saw it all going on about 400 yards ahead. As we advanced the barrage lifted gradually. Machine guns on either flank kept up a continuous chant. Three bofors about the centre of the advance gave us our direction by firing tracer simultaneously. The two outer tracers converging on the centre one forming an arrow.

We reached our objection at 4am and dug in smartly. Me being number 2 on the Bren Gun. Not a very enviable position. Dave Parr was No.1. At 5.30 we had to `stand to' while the Major made an inspection. Bruce Peterson reminded me of "Ole Bill" looking for a better 'ole, crouched in his slit trench. It was terrifically cold and at 6am we up and marched about 5 mile back to the trucks for breakfast.
Tiny Freyberg ('Blood & Guts') gave a speech to the officers and sergeants and we got the oil about going places later from them.

27th September... Arrived back at Bir el Arab about 3pm. Saw a lot of knocked out German tanks on the way, also Ity's. Big tank transporters were taking them forward to let the Div. Cav. and Shermans have a lash at them. Also the new armoured cars, which are a great job. Had a bo-peep at them back at Maadi and they have everything. Firepower, mobility and armour and the biggest tyres I've ever seen. Cost 600 pound for four. Also saw Sherman tanks the Germans had captured and we got back from them.

> (Hot and tired the troops arrived back and almost as one man made for the cool surf. For the next three days the men practically lived in the water. Doctor Fletcher and his staff completed the typhus inoculations.) (O)

Nelson and Dave Parr on leave in Christchurch, New Zealand.

30th September... Today another fire and movement exercise, wherein I lost a lot of sweat. I also took part in a hand grenade practice. 69s for knocking them silly and 36s for knocking them cold. I threw a 36 but too low and I lay flat waiting on the bang for what seemed hours but really only three seconds. Shrapnel whizzed but no one was hit.

3rd October... Packed up this morning and left by transport for Amiriya, a transit Pommy camp. Stayed here for a day.
That night I met my cousin Pat Price and we promptly got tight.
Ran into a barb wire fence and tore a hole in my left leg, which evened up the cut I got on my right leg at the Red Sea. (refer p21)

> (The safeguarding of health and of secrecy had their place among preparations for the move. The usual precautions against malaria of the warm season in Italy were ordered before embarkation and the risk of pestilence during the Italian winter was countered by the issue of warm clothing, [two pairs of boots, New Zealand winter underclothing, battle dress and leather jerkins] and bivouac shelters, by

inoculation against typhus, and by provision of mobile laundries and disinfectors. The removal of signs, titles and badges extinguished the most obvious means of identifying the New Zealanders and enforced in the minds of the men the need for security.) (I)

(Their ship carried the new clothing items which was issued to Nelson etc after they were settled in Camp near Taranto, in Italy about 31st October 1943. (T)

5th October... Next day we packed up and left for Alexandria by Pommy transport. Big ten tonners which held 30 chaps with all their gear. Arrived at Alexandria after passing a huge artillery concentration of captured Hun and Ity guns. A hang of a lot of gear, and thousands of Wogs encamped nearby. We were driven right to the wharf, debussed and then marched onto a ferry which held about a thousand chaps. About one hour later we climbed the gang plank of the "MV Reina del Pacifico", a South American liner of 17 thousand tons. (no photo found. T)
Had a hang of a job finding our proper bunk area on B deck.

Went out on deck for a breath of fresh air and a look around.
Alexandria is a huge naval base and there were lots of ships of the freshly capitulated Ity navy standing close inshore. They looked good. There were two other liners not quite as big as ours, embarking the rest of 6th Brigade troops and one could see lines of khaki crawling up gang planks. Balloon barrages overhead and trucks and carriers being loaded onto Liberty-ships.
I swung the old hammock and slept soundly after having a good tea of our first Pommy rations.

6th October... Set sail from Alexandria and travelled north-west all day. We did not know where we were going, but a fair idea it was Italy. We got the `oil' this afternoon that we were going to Taranto in the heel of Italy, where the British navy had a big raid some months ago.

7th October... Sailed on serenely all day and the next with the Libyan coast on our port beam. Met Harold Rogers on board and had a good old yarn. He looked fit.

8th October... That night near dark we came in sight of land, presumably Italy. A high mountain on the left and some white stone buildings. At dusk we passed a convoy of over 30 ships going in a southerly direction, looked a great sight.

--oo0Ooo--

HANDKERCHIEF posted to son Trevor from Egypt. Actually is of beige cloth with light blue Pyramids, edging and saddle cloth.

--o0o--

ITALY 1943-44:

9th October... Today saw us sailing up the welt of Italy and at 9am we dropped anchor in the roadstead of Taranto. A magnificent sight. The city of 750,000 with high buildings along the water-front and many dozens of all kinds of ships in the bay. A real league of nations. Balloon barrages were up, as Italy was only one month our ally. Unfortunately, our platoon was kept behind, while the rest of the boys disembarked and marched to their new camp.

Going ashore at Taranto

We were the baggage party and unloaded all the gear, and what a job. Jeeps and motor bikes, tents, and all the rest of the gear required by the Infantry. At 12 mid-night we arrived on shore and unpacked the barge. Gear everywhere. No transport was able to be had so we had to bunk down on the wharf, after a cup of tea, bully beef and biscuits. Tired as blazes and wet with sweat.

A map of ITALY shows the **City of TARANTO**, at the instep of the boot shape of Italy. Nelson mentions **Taranto, Crispiano, Martina, Montemesola**, **Brindisi, Bari,** and his military camp at **Mass Santa Teresa, north of Taranto,** where he was camped for five weeks.

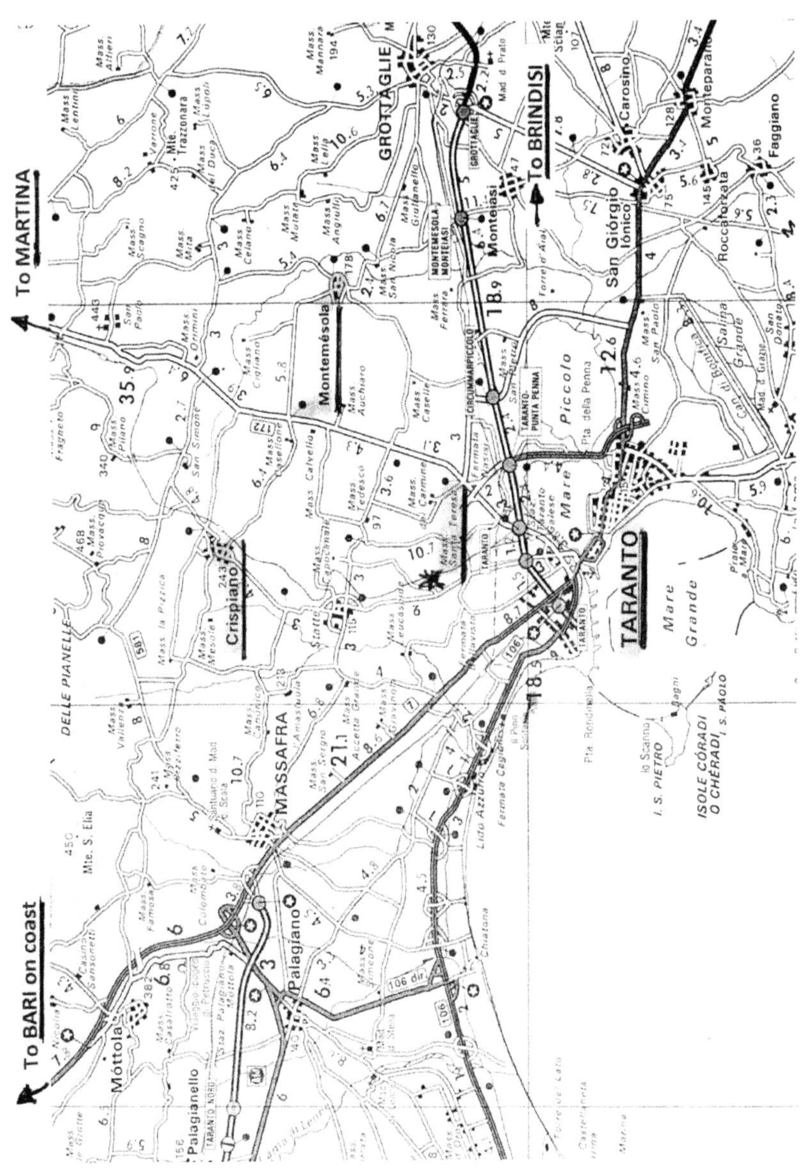

TARANTO : The entrance to Taranto Harbour features a Turning Bridge, half open above and closed below. The lower photo also shows Aragonese Castle at the far side of the harbour entrance.

Nelson sent two photo booklets with many colour photos of Taranto and district to wife Lillian. They still exist. (T).

10th October... Day dawned with plenty of dew and shivering Kiwis. During the night packing cases 'accidentally' burst and tins of fruit, milk, bacon, coffee etc, disappeared.

We weren't slow and supplies of our section were built up considerably, including candles. No sense in being backward in coming forward. After a stroll around the wharf, we landed a truck and moved off to our new camp amongst olive trees and rock walls, and plenty of Italians only too willing to sell grapes and nuts.

11th October... Began the day with a lecture from Major Smith on treatment of Italians. Not to be friendly but firm and polite. Built a rock path to our cookhouse in the afternoon. Hard work. Began to rain so I stripped off to bathing suit and boots. Boys laughed, but my pants were dry and theirs were wet.

> (Orders were received to move to a camp 160 miles from Taranto. On 11 Oct, Col Fountaine and 2Lt McLean left to inspect La Torre, a small village not far from Lucera. (O)

12th October... Our Officer Alf McLean took No 11 (platoon) out on a route-march. Three hours and one hour of lectures. Watched sheep and goats being herded through the almond trees. Lots had small bells attached to their neck. There was a continual jingle. In afternoon went on a compass course. Same at night.

13th October... Went on leave to Taranto with Bob Henderson, Dave Parr and Jim Gemmel. Walked right into town, about 5 miles. Saw lots of Ity soldiers on the way digging pipe lines. Shabby uniforms. Pommies were road repairing.

Taranto was a huge city and hundreds of all classes on the streets. On the way in I saw lots of bomb damage by RAF bombers. Buildings split in two, railway carriages on their sides, telephone wires lying and hanging everywhere, debris lying everywhere. Stories of buildings gaping could see wallpaper and even some chairs still in position. Went over swing-bridge that opens to let ships through. Pulled into a stationery shop and bought a postcard folder of Taranto for Lin. (see pages 32/33)

Along the street I bought a couple of Xmas cards for Trevor and Marlene, also a tin to hold soap and razor blades.

Had a cup of coffee and chocolate buns in a coffee stall. Looked around town and had our dinner, of a tin of Bully and two slices of bread, on a seat in a tram. Ity boys keen on Bully. Hardly any meat in towns. Saw a long food queue at one place. Poor looking people. Very little in way of eats in town, except almond toffee and marshmallow cakes.

(Is this an 'Ity Garry' ... T.)

Came back to camp in an Ity Garry and pinched 2 tins from dump. Cost 10/- ... 2/6 each way for the Garry.

Had to get out and push Garry up hills as horse was so thin. The old Ity pushed too. Got some elastic for Lin, cost 5/-.

Fairly soon after arriving in Italy, Nelson must have wanted to communicate with the Italians, especially on day trips into town. This is his writing of handy words to know, and how to pronounce them ….

WAR Date

Slowly	(Adagio)	Ah-dah-jo
I do not understand.	(non capisco)	non: ka: pis: koh
have you understood?	(Capitò?)	Kah-pee-tòh
Tea.	(tè)	tāy
Coffee.	(caffe)	kah-fay
water	(acqua)	Ah-kwah.
Wine	(vino)	Vee-noh
Bread	(pane)	Pah-nay
Egg	(uova)	ooh-oh-vah
Fish	(pesce)	pess-kay
Meat	(carne)	Kar-nay
Woman	(donna)	Don-nah
There is	(c'è)	chay
yes.	(si)	see
No	(no)	noh
one	(uno)	ooh-noh
two	(due)	doo-ay
three	(trē)	tray
four	(quattro)	kwa-troh
five	(cinque)	chin-kway
six	(sei)	say-ee
seven	(sette)	set-tay
eight	(otto)	oh-toh
nine	nove	no-vay
ten	dieci	dee-ay-chee

14th October... Have to be up at 6.30am, shaved and dressed for our 7.30 breakfast time. Went out on section instruction, attack and defence, did some ambushes and crawled through scrub. Rocks hard on knees.

15th October... Did some washing and built up our bivvy with rocks. Great improvement. Afternoon was pay parade and then away out on a compass course. 6.30pm another compass course in the dark. Reached objective 1300 paces and returned. Number two section got lost for a while.

16th October... Duty Day. Went on picket at midnight. Dave Parr and I heated a tin of herrings and had a feed. Went away up gully on my own and wrote 7 pages to Lin and began writing up diary. Back at 11am, shaved and had dinner and on picket 12 noon to 1pm. Aired blankets and in evening drank Ity wine with "Bludge" McEwan, Dave, Bert Davidson, Bruce Paterson & Keith Campbell. Head a bit giddy and legs wobbly. Don't like Ity wine much.

17th October... Sunday, Church parade 9am. Howard Stenhouse played on cornet, "Oh God our help in ages past." Was good. Football match between 12 & 11 platoon at 11am. Lay in bivvy, ate grapes and wrote to Mum and finished Lin's letter. 11 Platoon beat 12 Platoon by 3 to nil. Dave and I got 3 jerry-cans of water from about 1 mile away. Got pretty heavy. Squared up tent and oiled Bren magazines and put them at head of bivvy. Had tummy ache from grapes. Good all the same.

18th October... Went out on a frugal. Did three attacks under live ammo. Pretty tough going. Not as fit as I thought. Platoon formations. Bought some grapes from an Ity.

19th October... Went on leave to Taranto with Dave Parr, Jack Wylie & Jim Gemmell. Walked so far then got a ride by lorry. Had a few wines and dinner. Bought a fountain pen, a broach, and a purse, each for Lin & Marlene and a pocketknife for Trevor, (never saw this pocketknife. Mum must have thought it too dangerous for a 6 year old and she probably gave me something else. T) also a small lamp and a wine flask, some photos to send to Mum and some buttons for battledress. Had a good day's scouting. Rumours of going in to stink soon. Don't fancy the idea much but if we have too ... let's go.

#11 Platoon: Nelson front left, sorry, don't know others. 18/10/43

20th October... Went out on company manoeuvres all morning. Practiced advancing and defensive positions. In afternoon did washing and Dave and I fixed up our kerosene lamps. At night went to YMCA Open Air Cinema, *"Charlie Chan at the Races."* Kerosene lamps OK. Ate grapes.

21st October... Away on a route-march, all day. 12 miles. Formation attack all the way to village of 'Crispiano'. Six miles there through olive groves and orchards of almond and fig trees. Very stony. Arrived at village at 11.30am and collected wood for boiling billy.

Marched through streets and all population of men, women & kids turned out to see us. Very thrilling. Was in shorts and battle order, must have seemed strange to Italians. I believe we were the first English troops to march through the village, ever, as inhabitants seemed so excited, calling out "English! English!" Had dinner and gave kiddies scraps. They were thin and ravenous. Picked marmalade jam out of tins and licked their fingers. Bought half a cup of plonk. (wine) One wee chap and I got on well. He was dirty and had a sniffly nose but nice mannered.

Marched back along railway line. Very hot in cuttings of line. Sweat dripping freely. Drank plonk at night. On picket from 12 to 2am and again 12 to 2pm tomorrow. Camp at where we are now is called "Massa Santa Teresa" about 5 miles inland from Taranto the chief naval base for southern Italy.
After tea had a nattering session round the campfire. The veno passed round and then Mr Miller got out his swanny whistle and a sing song developed. Mr McLean, Les Kevern R.S.M, Dave Welsh Sgt, and most of our crowd were present.

22nd October... Day dawned very hot and calm. Went on frugal. Waddy attacking and then taking a strong point by sections. Good views of Taranto. Lay in bivvy in afternoon and half slept.
Manoeuvres again tonight. No 11 are `Enemies'. 23rd arriving all day. Transport coming up 24th. Supposed to move out to transit camp on 29th. Manoeuvres washed out. Went to pictures, *"The Wolf Man."* Pretty spooky. Big crowd there. Lots of 5th Brigade chaps.

23rd October... Had a pretty easy morning. Cleaned Bren magazines and Bren and Rifle. Cleaned up around "table" under Olive tree. Mr Miller made a camp oven out of tin. Ate nuts. Went to bed early. Dave feeling pretty crook. Flu. "Mae" hurt his shoulder at football. I'm in team to play tomorrow. Tonight is anniversary of big El Alamein, Egypt, successful second attack of 23 Oct 1942.

24th October... Awoke early and put on fire for shaving water. Wrote to Lin most of day. Joe Richardson and I went and got grapes along the road. Big bombing raid on up north. 58 Flying Fortresses passed over at 10 o'clock. Came back in dribs and drabs. One putting a trail of smoke out of port engine. Had game of football, two quarter hour spells. Was winded and got legs cut about on stones and hard ground. No more football for me.
Going on picket 6 to 8pm. Very stiff.

25th October... Went out to aerodrome, nine miles from Taranto on Brindisi Road, with Lft McLean and Sgt Major Kevern. Had a wonderful day. Hitched and hiked there with 1 water-car, 4 trucks, 2 jeeps and a water-car to Taranto. Truck over bridge, then Tommy parachutist jeep to aerodrome at 60 mph all the way. Thrilling.
Met Jim Hammill and Ron? his pilot. Jim is NFO A. G. (?) Flies recci-planes up as far as Venice. 'Marauders'. Saw Fortresses and Bostons, Liberators, Spitfires, Hurricanes and Mitchells. Big raid on Austria. Saw 60 Fortresses leaving to bomb Messerschmitt's Aero Factory in Austria. Previously bombed 140 Messerschmitt on the ground and destroyed them.
Had dinner and afternoon tea and came back to Taranto by pommie truck with 8 pongos and 3 sailors off monster that bombarded Naples. It had two 15 inch guns. Got a ride from Taranto by truck, changed to another truck and finished up in a jeep in which was General King, 2 Lft Colonels and 1 Lft, besides Mr McLean, Les Kevern and me. Quite a load.

26th October... Went for route-march out main Bari road, round toward Taranto and back by an old Monastery at 11.30am. Free afternoon and manoeuvres tonight at 6.30 pm.

27th October... Went out on Battalion manoeuvres all morning. Marched about 3000 yards and took up a gun line. Anti-tank gun protection. Read in afternoon.

On picket at 4 to 5pm and again 5 to 7 in the morning.

28th October... Cleaned up around tree today. Swept "table and floor", washed clothes, cleaned bivvy, drank veno for stimulant, went with Dave for a load of firewood, wrote to Vera and had a good time in general.

ITALIAN FARMERS AT WORK

Being raised on a farm, Nelson must have thought this archaic. (T)

29th October... Sent air-graph to Vera and cablegram to Lin ... "Am well and fit. Hope kiddies are well. Love from Daddy." Rained. Locals here fixing ditching system.

Night of 28th/29th was awful. Lightning, the which I have never seen before. Brilliant and pretty well continuous and thunder like 25 pounders going off. Rained all night and most of the next day. Bivvy was dry so stayed in bed. Dave got up and made breakfast. Some chaps flooded out of tents.

30th October... Rained all night and most of day. Everything damp now, if not wet. Dave got up and brought me breakfast in bed. Two mornings with breakfast in bed. Lay till 10.30. Got up and made toast and boiled billy. This afternoon got issued with leather "jerkin", 1 pair extra socks, extra blanket, shirt, singlet and underpants. Can't get washing dry no-how. Transport arrived today. Was 15 days on the way.

Liberty ships (American) called at Malta for three days, not allowed on shore and again at Catalina. Lived on Bully and Biscuits whole time. Monday is 1st November. At home daffodils will be about had it. Apple tree will have bloomed and potatoes just above the ground. Wondering if Lin has had to hill them. Hens should be laying well and plenty earwigs around. Strawberries will be kids delight, also raspberries.

31st October... Arose early, day very good. Put very damp clothes and blankets out to dry. Put up tent for Major, and with Dave and Bert carried rocks for truck track. Wrote to Lin and Mum per air-graph. Re-erected bivvy.

1st November... First day of Winter. Very hot. Went on an all-day route march across country, rocks and scrub, valleys and stone walls, to the village of Montemesola about eight miles away, about 17 miles there and back. Was very tired and hot. Had dinner there, got wine and bought it home in our water bottles.

Had a nattering session at night, great show. Got rid of thirty-two bottles of plonk. Over thirty of us. Finished with Dave putting me in bed. Slept in my new battledress which was issued last night.

2nd November... Went on frugal to take up a gun line this morning and two hours same thing this afternoon. On offensive patrol tonight in sections. Very stupid. In sandals and muddy.

3rd November... Wharf party of 13 left on job. Dave and I got leave but didn't go on leave. Got two jerry-cans of water. I got load of firewood and then loafed around. Tiring.

4th November... Had a very easy day. Went for water in morning. Sewed 6th Brigade patch onto new battledress and put up NZ titles. Got paid in 100, 50, 10, 5, 2 and 1 Lire notes. Played cards at night, supper of tea and toast. Lt and Mr Keown went for load of wood !!!!

Nelson posted son Trevor these two bank notes, marked **<u>'Allied Military Currency'</u>**, dated 1943. They are blank on the other side.

5th November... Went on leave to Bari, about 50 mile north of Taranto, by Red Cross truck belonging to 5th Brigade. Big city about 3 times the size of Taranto. One and a half million people there. Had a good look around. Bought Lin Views and chain for pendant.

> (Mail from New Zealand arrived regularly but few parcels reached the camp. In other respects, the men welcomed the change from the desert.) (O)

6th November... Finished letter to Lin. Duty platoon today. Cleaned a few malaria pills and ointment containers. Lay in bivvy. Rained fairly heavy. Carried summer issue of clothing down to Q.M.

7th November... Sunday. Got up pretty late, shaved and did damn all. Made a cover for McEwan's tommy gun. Helped Dave to clean the Bren. Paraded for lecture on Eighth Army front. Wrote airgraph to Lin. Rain threatening. Plenty of aeroplanes flying over camp daily. Spitfires, Lightenings, Hurricanes, Douglas DC3 Transports, Bostons, Mitchells, Liberators and Fortresses.

8th November... Did very little. Packed up in readiness to move to new camp. Sent airgraph to Mum and Lin. Checked ammunition for cracked cases.

ON THE MOVE NORTH TO THE FRONT.

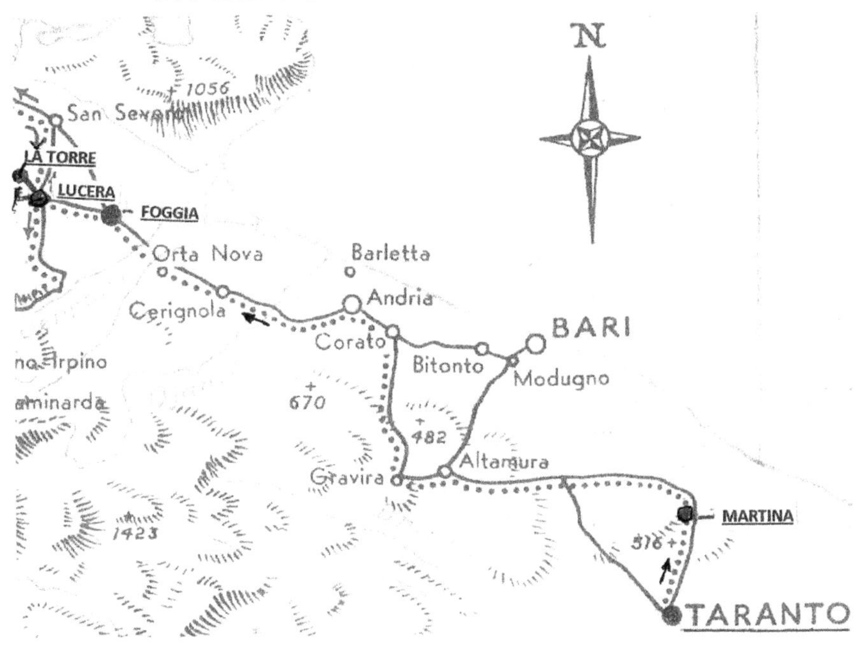

NELSON'S TRAVELS IN ITALY .... Map # 1:
.... FOLLOW THE DOTS FROM TARANTO ....

9th November... Up at 5 o'clock. Packed and rolled up bivvy with rest of 3 section. (Advance Party) Had breakfast 6am at Battalion.

Loaded trucks (3) and left 7am. Slow ride for a good way and passed through many villages and towns. Lots of skinny looking kids, funny houses and stone walls. Passed through Martina, world famous for its wines. I rode in truck for about 100 miles until we had dinner of bread, butter and jam. No tea. Then I got on top of cab with Dave. We stuck it out all the way, although terrifically cold. Refuelled at Foggia and then entered the city.

Very battered about by bombs. Practically flat. Streets full of debris, rocks, pieces of houses and also hundreds of skinny, very dirty and scantily clad children of all ages. A heart rendering sight. All trying to cadge cigarettes, apparently to sell them to get food. Saw smashed up railway engines and carriages and blown up bridges. Passed miles of convoys on way and also refugees returning to their homes in mule and donkey carts, with furniture and bedding tied all over the place.

Passed an advanced aerodrome and eventually arrived at camp site at Le Torre at 4.30pm. 150 mile behind us and only 50 mile from front fighting line where 8th Army is going hammer and tongs, knee deep in mud and slush. We can hear guns and bombing in early morning and in the evenings. Dull booming. Pitched our bivvies on damp ground and long grass. Very damp and cold in the mornings.

10th November... Began the day by having a shifty around. Found an Ity well, also an orchard with 1/2 quince and 1/2 apple type fruit. (Not bad to eat but a bit sour.) Helped build a culvert from road to get our trucks in. Very cold day. Dug drainage ditch around area.

Shifted bivvys into company area. Rained. Found a tomato patch and got down on the tomatoes. About two dixies' full. Cooked them and had them with biscuits for dinner. Very good.

Traded 2 packets of cigarettes for two eggs. Getting 10 tomorrow among 5 of us. Will have a feed later when we get enough. Went to bed early. Very tired. At La Torre about 20 miles from Foggia.

11th November... Anniversary of Armistice ....
(Cessation of hostilities of WW1 .... 11am, 11 day, 11 month, 1918.)

Got up at 7am after good sleep on straw. Shaved big whisker. Had breakfast and began work at 8.30 spreading metal from trucks for road into area until noon. Went with Joe to get Ity plow and 2 bullocks with Ity Teamster. Funny wee plough. Began area drainage at 3 and finished by 4pm. Got nine eggs this morning for 4/6 and traded an old shirt this afternoon for 12 more. Got an issue of cigarettes and matches and Wog chocolate. Cost 61 Lire. Good food and plenty of it. Issue of white wine tonight. Sworn off it. Dave and I lay in bivvy and read. Supper of tea and biscuits.

> (With less than half its force in position around Lucera, 2 NZ Division was ordered forward to a concentration area between Furci and Gissi.) (location pages 48/49 map) (B)

12th November... Began the day at 8 o'clock unloading trucks and making road. Bert and I went for water to well before morning tea of coffee and milk and 2 biscuits. Made table and prepared tomatoes for dinner. Had dinner of toast, 1 egg poached and fried tomatoes. (Goodio!) Dave Welsh, Bert, Keith, Mo and I went up to Ity hut in afternoon after marking our bivvy area and got a pair of scissors, bit of wire, bit of sandstone for sharpening knives, enamel plate for frying pan and made a frame for same to act as handle. Also got a bellows to blow up the fire. Rigged it up. Wrote to Lin at night. Had tea and biscuits for supper. Looks like rain. Saw 60 bombers going up to front in the morning and 24 in the afternoon. Heard the bombs landing and also the heavy guns. Boys think a big `push' is on.

13th November... Helped to put a gravel road into Support Group this morning and had a look around homestead. Big show. Four cages of Muskrats, big hairy things about as big as a cat, with a long slimy looking tail.

Cooked 1 egg each for boys in frying pan in oil. Tried to get some pork fat. Some chaps tried to go to Naples but truck broke down.

Very disappointed. Put in 1/6 each for pig and had pork (roasted) spuds, peas and gravy, apricots and sauce for tea. Best feed I've had in Egypt and Italy. Cold pork for dinner tomorrow.
The rest of our crowd arriving tomorrow. Yarned in bivvy and wrote to Lin at night. Very cold.

> (A cold wind was blowing and the skies were threatening. Before nightfall rain began and the staging area soon became a sea of mud. There was no change on the 14th and 15th and once again bivvys were flooded and bedding soaked. During the 14th and 15th the unit transport and the Anti-tank Platoon re-joined the Battalion) (O)

14th November... Going to within 5 miles of the front line in about a weeks' time. Mr McLean arrived back from a visit to the front line. He is staying here until rest of chaps arrive today. He said there was snow at the front, frozen hard. Things was quiet but our airforce giving Gerry hell. Said one village was bombed and 200 civilians killed. Dave and I went and helped erect cooks tent, which had blown down in the night, in high wind. Tins scattered everywhere. Peas split and flour tins.

Boys arrived about 2pm. Trucks everywhere. High wind and raining. Boiled up five billies of tea for them. Chas turned up. Just missed me at Messa Santa Teresa by one day. Had a good natter to him in our bivvy. Looks just the same old Chas.
Helped to unload cooks truck of hotboxes, dixies and water tins.
Feverish activity all over the area. Chaps carting straw to their bivvy site, others erecting bivvies etc, and cooks getting tea ready. Chas was in air-raid at Bari before disembarking. Saw much Ack Ack and one driver of our trucks was killed by enemy rear gunner. Stick of bombs missed transport area, but rear gunner connected.

15th November... Went on route march up hill. Pretty hard going. Mud stuck to boots making them about 10lbs each. Away an hour.

Checked over Bren mags and own ammo. Issued with scarf and gloves. Getting ready for move up to front line, to take over from 8th Indian Division.

THE FRONT LINE as at 15 November 1943
And the front line position 9 days before.

(Nelson's part of the Army was still at Le Torre on this date. See right hand side of map. T)

PIAT GUN to be carried on mule.
Rations to be carried on mules.
Sent Xmas airgraphs to Dave P, Lin, Mrs Thomas and Vera. (p 45)
Have to wear battledress from now on. Sounds like the Infantry will do all the work. Armour no use in hills and mud.

16th November... Left Le Torre a sea of mud en-route per trucks for the River Sangro, winter line of Gerry. Travelled 180 mile and had to stop at 2am and sleep on road beside trucks. Awfully muddy. Trucks put on chains and still have them on.

NELSON'S TRAVELS IN ITALY ... Map # 2: 16 Nov '43

Follow the dots from La Torre. Also see enlarged map page 49.

17th November... Started on the second day's journey after a hot breakfast, in sound and flash observance of enemy and our guns. Two bridges blown so had an all-day wait until transport cleared itself. The night previously Gerry had a go at blowing the third bridge with a night patrol of 90 men, but were repulsed with the loss of 50 men. Graves all along the roadside.

Arrived B Ech at 2am and proceeded to sort out individual gear.

A hell of a job in a muddy creek bed.

> (Wireless silence was imposed during the move forward on the 17th to relieve the Indians after dusk on the 18th.
>
> After the convoy had passed through Termoli and turned inland, demolitions and traffic jams forced the lorries to halt many times and slowed down progress. There were plenty of signs of recent fighting ... blown bridges, shell torn

homes, abandoned and burnt-out vehicles. Here and there were the graves of British and German soldiers. After dark the going became even slower. They stopped for a cup of tea and two hours later the convoy resumed its journey, finally stopping for the night on a side road leading to Gissi. The men slept in their trucks or on the damp ground.) (O)

An Enlarged Section of MAP # 2 on page 48:

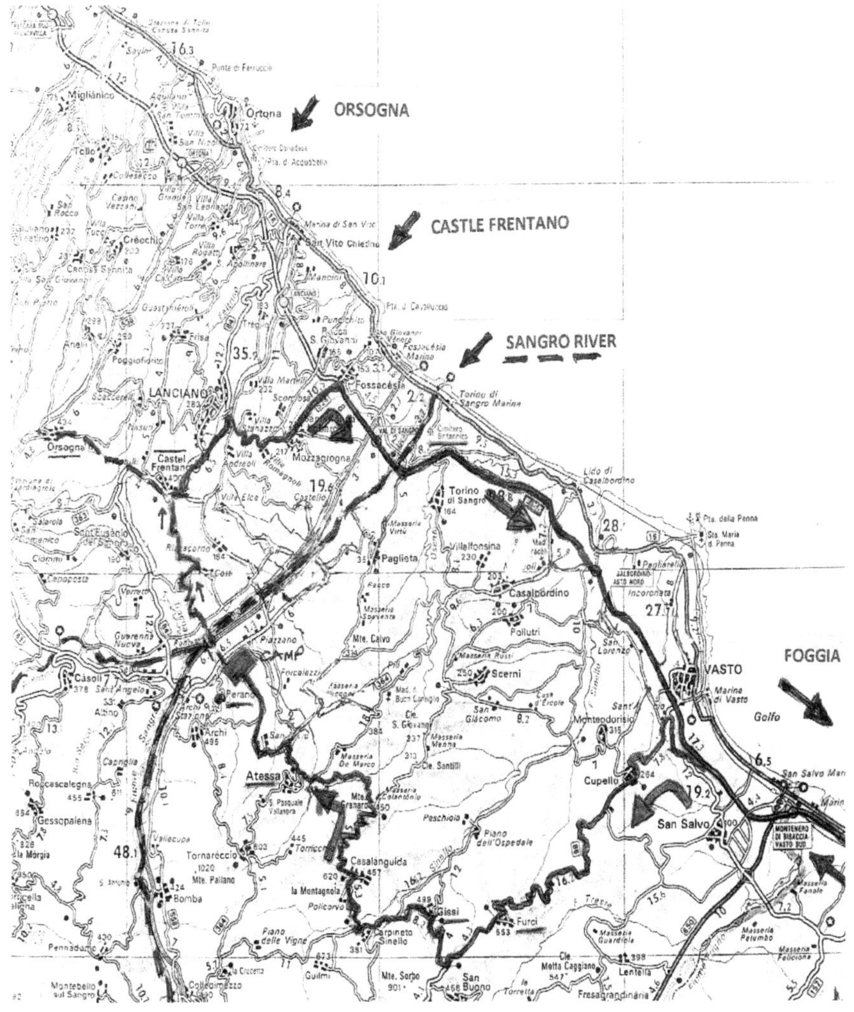

(Ahead of them lay a 6 mile march over the hills to the new sector. Except for essential vehicles all transport was to remain in the river bed, and this meant that all gear had to be carried. Before the companies set out the cooks provided a hot meal … the second in 36 hours. By dawn the march had been completed and the troops were sheltering beneath olive trees about four miles from the Sangro.) (O)

The CHRISTMAS AIRGRAPH mentioned 15 November 1943

The address must NOT be typewritten.

TO:- Mrs Nelson Price.
17 Wilton Street,
Invercargill
Southland.
New Zealand.

PASSED BY CENSOR No. 304

Write the message very plainly below this line.

Sender's Address 471269. PTE N. PRICE. B Company 26 Battalion 2NZEF MEF

CHRISTMAS GREETINGS FROM THE MEDITERRANEAN -
- And a Happy new year from yours lovingly... Nel, xxxxx
(in, don't forget to show The Kiddies the stick figures. I've added)

This space should not be used.

18th November... Under Fire. Moved off on foot at 3am and marched until 6am. Very strenuous and shoulders ached like blazes under heavy pack load, also carried pick and occasionally gave Dave a spell carrying the Bren gun. Arrived at dispersal area and dug in fast, to beat the daylight, in an Olive grove. We were under enemy observation. Stayed put all day and at night moved out at 5pm in single file and arrived on forward slope facing enemy and dug in at 8pm. Only got 1 hours sleep. Very muddy and claggy.

> (The 18th saw the first tank action undertaken by the New Zealanders … the attack on Perano.) (B)
>
> (Except for reconnaissance parties which went down to the river, the men kept under cover for the rest of the day so that the enemy would not see fresh troops moving in.) (O)

19th November...Very cold and began to rain early morning. Got pretty wet and went into cellar of Ity house and cleaned weapons. Slept for three hours. Gerry mortars and 88s very busy all day. They killed at least 6 chaps belonging to 24th and wounded 9 others. Spandau fire, very close. Two patrols from A Company tried to cross River Sangro but left it too late before dawn. Ten Platoon, B Company out all day on standing patrol. Rotten thing, a mortar.
Big, 8th Army barrage, also Vickers and Spandau fire, very close.

> (Company sectors were selected and by 5pm the troops set out on foot towards the river. By half past 7 they had reached their positions and were digging in. The ground was wet and soggy, after recent rain. B Company 26th, (Nelson's) was on the lower ground. Battalion HQ was set up in a house not far behind.

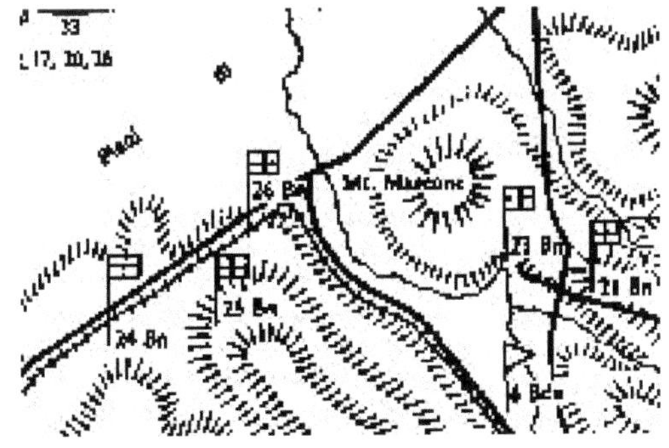

Defensive positions were completed by 11pm.
The 26th Battalion was holding a 300 yard front, near Monte Marcone with 25th Battalion on its left and the Apello River, a tributary to the Sangro, to its right.) (O)

BOGGED TRUCK NEAR THE SANGRO RIVER .....

Manhandling a truck bogged at the Sangro

(Lt-General Bernard Freyberg (a New Zealander) was in charge of the 2nd NZ Expeditionary Force 1939-1945. He formed the plans to remove Hitler's troops. Hitler's orders were to hold the Gustav Line, running through mountainous territory between the Sangro River in the east and the Garigliano River (at Cassino) in the west of the country. The Allies had to fight this very difficult terrain during the Italian winter. The New Zealanders, bolstered by the 19 Indian

Brigade, got the left side of the push to the towns of Orsonga and Castlefrentano. (F)

(At daylight on the 20th the troops examined their new surroundings. The narrow flat occupied by the 26th was heavily cultivated with olive trees, vineyards and orchards, providing plenty of natural cover. The apple trees were soon stripped of their fruit. Peasants and their families undeterred by the shelling, still occupied their homes. On the north side of the river a marshy ground ran up into a series of sharply defined hills. Seven wet and unpleasant days followed, and the river was soon in flood and uncrossable.) (O)

(The Kiwis used the period 19-27 November to prepare for a major assault across the Sangro River. During this time they sent 44 patrols toward the German lines. The patrols ranged from 2 men to a platoon. The majority went at night. (B)

20th November... In slitty all day, hung pretty close to ground. Gerry shelling and mortaring our positions regularly. 24th Battalion got a hammering whilst C Company lost their cookhouse.

Our barrage blasting away all day, ranging for the attack which was to come. 14 Bostons dive bombing all day a village 5 mile away, across the Sangro. (probably Orsogna or Castelfrentano)
Terrific spectacle. Had birds eye view.

Our patrols very active and fighting across the Sangro. Dave and Jack Wylie went on night patrol, to try to cross river, but was too deep. Got wet up to the waist.

Nelson wrote this POEM ......

His dairy does not note when he wrote it ... but on 20 November 1943 he was ***"in a slitty all day"***.
He may have written it while in the Italian hospital in 1944, or maybe even after he returned home.

IT COSTS NO MORE

To enjoy the rich flavour and the high nutritive quality of

MILLARS
MILK-MADE BREAD.

"Italy, back in forty-three,
In a 'Slitty,' 'neath a tree,
I sat and tried to eat my lunch
Of biscuits, very hard to crunch.

"They make 'em hard so they will keep,
And pack 'em round inside a jeep,
We get 'em issued, day by day,
From August to the month of May.

"This day in Italy, forty-three,
Thoughts of home came back to me,
I thought of 'Millars' milk-made bread,'
'Good things to eat' came to my head.

"There drifted past my vision's gaze,
Sponges, cream-cakes in a haze,
Vienna, pan, and Scotch bread, too,
And girdle scones, as my dream grew.

"It wasn't long, it was a shame,
And those hard biscuits were to blame,
My dream it went, as good things do,
And left me, with my thoughts to rue.

"So, in that 'Slitty,' 'neath a tree,
A lesson, hard, was shown to me,
That when the peace comes to this land,
I'll eat more 'Millars' bread,' it's grand."

—Contributed by Nelson Price

This was printed in the 31 August 1944 issue of the Southland Daily News on page 1. Nelson had returned to Invercargill 13 June 1944.

--o0o--

21st November...
Took up standing Patrol on banks of Sangro.
Plenty mortar and 88s flying about, also 25 pounders belting hill across river. Dug in smartly. Ate grapes, apples and figs and biscuits. Observed enemy slope for signs of enemy. Our mortar opened up about 4pm on Gerry dug-outs and made them scatter.

22nd November... In Ity cellar all day. Big attack to be launched at 12pm but cancelled after getting everything packed up. Felt like a bust balloon. Indian attack successful but gave ground.

23rd November... Slept in cellar. Stayed here. Wrote letter to Lin.

(Heavy rain after dusk on the 23rd caused the tank supported thrust to be abandoned, and the troops settled down to wait until the level of the river fell.) (O)

24th November... Much shelling for two days. Some pretty close, landing near slit trench, nearly got Del Fea who dived in on top of 'Ghandi'. (Fred Alderton) Del was on picket. Lay in cellar, ate apples and slept, played cards and swore at chaps for moving about so much in daylight. Half our crowd moved back 2 miles for spell.

25th November... Went for spell to back area. Had wash and shave as guest of Pte McIntosh Aturehua, who is driver of 'staghound', a new armoured car. Wrote to Lin, Mum and Harold ... airgraphs.

26th November... Issue of chocolate and cigarettes. Big show supposed to be on tonight. Lay low and rested. Aired blankets. Issue of Rum. Examined all Bren mags and rifle. Big clean up. Attack again postponed.

(The powerful German defensive position was known as The Gustav Line with Casino it's pivot. The line covered the narrowest point of the Italian peninsula and was protected by large minefields and rivers that had been dammed to flood the valleys, and the mountains in the centre.

The NZ Division was first into action in Italy when it crossed the Sangro River on 27 November 1943. This was the right flank of the British 8th Army position under Montgomery facing the Gustav Line on the Adriatic coast. On the other side of the peninsular the American 5th Army was facing the Gustav Line at Cassino.) (W)

27th November... <u>FIRST ATTACK ... CROSSING THE SANGRO</u>

(Although the enemy manned a number of strongpoints on bluffs, his main defences were sited on a series of high ridges, the nearest of which lay about 6 miles away. This ridge, which ran parallel to the river, could be seen with the village of Castlefrentano, a prominent landmark, on it.) (O)

(About 1930 hours the lead troops marked the crossing points with stakes sunk into both banks. About 2130 hours the Kiwis silently started forward and began to cross the river. In total 2,000 men waded across. They crossed in various ways ... holding onto a taut wire that had previously been strung across... using wooden poles for support, or forming a chain with each man holding the rifle of the man next to him. The movement went smoothly and generally without notice. On the approach eight men from 21 Battalion were killed or wounded by a mine, but most reached the start line. On the right B-Co (Nelson) scrambled up the slippery slope, through the grape vines and reached point 217 without opposition, then 11 platoon (Nelson) went up the right hand side of the gully leading to the peak. B-Co escaped the minefield unharmed, then turned west towards the ridge line objective some 900 yards away. Numbers 10 and 11 platoons led the way with the men bunched up due to the darkness. They crossed a narrow valley, climbed on to the sharp ridge, and dug in, all without opposition.) (B)

Rested all day. Show on tonight for certain. Had tea at 6pm and another meal at 10pm. Started out on *'great adventure'* at 10.30pm and waded through mud for a couple of hours and assembled on river bank. Very cold and began crossing river with trousers rolled up above knees, at midnight or shortly after. Reached the farther banks after wading through four streams, the deepest above my knees and very swift. Pretty hard to keep upright. Ken Harvey stayed back. Wasn't strong enough to make the grade. Changed socks in pitch dark and reached start line at 2.45am. Barrage began then of 95 guns with 300 rounds apiece. Terrific row and flashes of shells exploding everywhere. Pretty tough going up hill and Gerry put up plenty flares and each time we had to go to ground. We took 5 Gerry prisoners who Keith Campbell and I shepherded back to 12 platoon. They were crew of either mortar or anti-tank gun. Were only half dressed and in the darkness looked fairly "bomb happy", flourishing white flags.

> (Unnerved by the severity of the bombardment, many of the German 65 Division, surrendered as soon as the New Zealanders got to close quarters. This fortuitous advantage of feckless opposition does not diminish the merit of the night's work by the 5 New Zealand battalions, which contained many men fighting their first action.
>
> (A Battalion comprises up to 1000 men. T)
>
> Wet-shod and chilled from the Sangro, they executed almost to a letter a plan of some complexity, finding their way over steep, difficult and unfamiliar country and rapidly organising to hold their gains against counter-attack.) (I)
>
> (The Kiwis suffered 150 casualties (killed or wounded) during the day, and took over 200 German prisoners.) (B)

28th November... Arrived at objective at 6.10am and started to dig in smartly but not smart enough, as C Co were advancing up a hill below ours and Gerry opened heavy fire with two Spandau's and an automatic tank gun firing tracer. Very ticklish spot. I thought our last day on earth had arrived. Dave opened up with Bren and quietened auto tank gun. Two of C Company killed. One hit and blown to pieces with anti-tank shell. Four wounded. C Co very lucky considering.

We dug like hell and I only had about 18 inches by 18 inches (45cm) to sit in all day. Just enough for cover. Dave and I opened up in afternoon and flattened two Gerrys trying to get back to their gun. Gerry dropped 4 times but stayed put 5th time. I fired 10 rounds, Dave fired a magazine and a half. Dug in more after dark.

29th November... Stood to at daybreak for half hour. Tiring picket all night. Dave went over to back area for spell. I took over Bren with Keith Campbell as 2 IC. (2nd in command) Got mortared pretty heavily. At 7pm advanced 1 1/2 miles and dug in on forward slope. Gerry had cleared out at midnight, we learnt later.

> (The winter temperatures and the rain and mud slowed them but the advance was steady. A night attack under artillery cover succeeded, and then a daylight attack to secure the strategic town of Castlefrentano. The German defence grew tougher as the towns of Orsogna and Guadiagrele were approached.
>
> Until January 1944 small gains were made, notably by 29 (Maori) Battalion whose objective was to reach the Orsogna-Ortona Road. The German's had had plenty of time to prepare their defences and it was clear the German forces were not going to yield ground lightly.) (W)

30th November... 6am had fresh bread and wine with very pleased Itys in village. (Castlefrentano) Advanced another mile to Ity house on top of hill, had dinner and Gerry started lobbing over dozens of mortars right on the target. Howard Stenhouse got shrapnel in legs and back of neck. Is OK. Joe Richardson got crook tummy.

I got inside Ity house, in kitchen and stayed put along with Kelly Ascot and Bert Davidson. Kelly's hat rolled in door and Kelly followed it smartly. One of 12 Platoon killed. Spandau opened up and gave us jiggery. Dug in 100 yards away at night.

> (The support arms finally reached 26 Battalion, which then, along with 24 Batt, moved 1.6 km towards Castlefrentano. Light enemy mortaring had little effect but 26 Battalion suffered one killed and seven wounded from mines. (B)

31st November...

Slept in slitty. Stood to at dawn. Woke mortar boys.

1st December... Went on daylight recci patrol with Mr McLean, all of 11 Platoon's number 3 section. Advanced 3000 yards up a muddy creek bed, bamboo and long grass. Got pretty wet and muddy. Right under noses of Gerry and his spandau. Gerry mortared hell out of us so kept well to cover. Observed wires at top of hill in front of Castlefrentano, a village of strategic importance.
Got back 3pm. Started to rain. Had wash and feed and felt OK again, but pretty shaken up and slept in house.

2nd Lieutenant
ALF McLEAN
(Nelson's commander)
He died at Cassino on 30 March 1944.

--o0o—

2nd December... Killed two geese and started to cook them along with spuds and cabbage but got hurried orders to advance, so gave them to cooks and they sent them up. Advanced about 2 miles under shell fire and Messerschmitts. Saw dead Gerrys and cows on road from bombing. Gerry mortared 24th boys just 200 yards on our right. Plenty of barbed wire and unset teller-mines. Dug in and stayed in Ity house. Ity pleased to see us and turned on apples. Brought in a porker pig, stunned and stuck it in the kitchen, for Mart Donnelly.

Blood all over the floor. We finished cooking and ate our geese, pretty good too. Two hours picket. Slept in house.

3rd December... Up at 4am, breakfast. 6am start. Advanced through village Castlefrentano & village in sorry state. Bombing very severe. Lots of Gerry gear lying about. Must have got out in a hurry. 24th and 25th Battalions pushed off objective of Orsogna by Gerry counter attack. Dug in twice on reverse slope. Gerry just over ridge

Castelfrentano

in front of 24th Battalion. Very active and mortaring. Shelling our road of approach. Plastered tanks broken down at foot of hill. They killed Bren carrier chap trying to repair carrier.

The hills of Orsogna and Castlefrentano towns. 29 Jan 1944.

4th December... Stayed put all day. Attack on Orsogna, put off on account Gerry having brought up 12 Mark VI tanks. Pretty deadly things. It fired on patrol of 24th and got some.

(Orsogna stood on rising ground across the valley from Castlefrentano. Between them lay the Moro, a boisterous stream, swollen by rain, leaving only the road for attack. (F)
(The Canadians were advancing on Ortona, a coastal village on the main road north from the Sangro River.) (F)

5th December... Stayed put all day. Did little. Had feed of chicken and cabbage and chicken soup. (Other units of NZ were in action)

6th December... My birthday. 33 Years.
Received 6 letters from Lin, 3 from Mum, an airgraph from Lin and Vera and a telegram from Mrs Thomas. It was she that sent remittance, not Lin as I thought. Attack again postponed to 2.30pm.

December 7, 2nd Anniversary of Pearl Harbour attack.

7th December... "GOING IN TODAY" Full scale show. 148 Spitfires as backing, also 400 rounds of 25 pounders per gun and over 150 guns. Should be some show. Maoris on our right. We (B Company) take over 24th positions. Box formation. Got up at 6am and had to go at 7.15 and do practice show for General Freyberg, to find out speed of advance of Infantry with all gear up. Twenty minutes for 500 yards agreed as fast enough. Brought diary up to date and prepared for afternoons attack. Not keen on daylight shows, but this one ought to be good as we have Sherman tanks in support... 26 ton tank, with 75mm gun. Was shown all over one yesterday by obliging crew. Colossal affairs but pretty awkward in soft going. Also `Pheasants'... 17 pounders.
Orsogna village, 4 miles away, still in enemy hands.

Barrage began at 1pm by 7th Field Regiment of Artillery. Maoris took objective and so did 24th which was village and vital road.

Sherman support? Like hell we did! During the night we had to evacuate owing to tanks not being able to get through, on account of roads blown up. Bad show. We advanced. Sgt fell into slitty.
26th Battalion in support, and dug in, in very forward position. Got plastered with 88s and mortars.

(Alexander Turnbull Library: DA-06507B-F)

A SHERMAN TANK of the NZ Armoured Brigade (right) along-side a German Panzer V1 Tiger tank.

Poor old Charlie Liffin was killed at 10.30 by air burst. Mortar had landed in a tree. Buried him this morning. He belonged to 1 section 11 Platoon, B Company.
26th, 24th and 28th were recalled at 2.30am as tanks couldn't make it. One platoon of 24th chopped about pretty badly. We dug in again 200 yards to rear of C Co and at day break returned to Ity house.

8th December... Tried to sleep but every time I was getting off a bomb or shell would land just outside the door. Airfire giving village a plastering half a mile away. Dive bombing and shooting up ammo dumps. Chicken for dinner. Had to go back to slitties at night to picket lines. Back to Ity house in morning.

(Attacks on Orsogna were abandoned. Instead, preparations were made to isolate the village by extending gains made by 23 Battalion. A fortnight went by before 26 Battalion were called in to take part in these operations. On the 8th, B and C Co's relieved the forward companies of 24 Battalion and were compelled to man trenches day and night. Wherever possible the rest of the Battalion occupied houses during the day and trenches at night.) (O)

9th December... Had a shave and began answering letters. Wrote one to Auntie Jess and one to Mrs Thomas. Cooked dinner of 8 chickens, cabbage and tatees. Boys pronounce it pretty good. Tanks opened up in village of Orsonga at 11am and pasted it for over two hours. Gerry threw back a lot of 88s, shaking our house on occasions. RAF hammering village all day and strafing. Smoke and flames rising from it. Tanks went back, probably for more shells.

Luftwaffe (German Airforce) on deck this morning, bombing our village and bridges. Saw a Spitty crash, after the pilot bailed out just in time. Lost one tank in flames, through AP shell. Direct hit. Driver killed, front gunner wounded. Tanks withdraw. They couldn't get in to village owing to houses blasted and mines.

10th December... Tanks reinforced 23 Battalion last night. Much fighting all night and 'arty' barrages too. We took up picketing lines as the previous night. Gerry pasted us with mortar fire. Probably heard the tankies working on broken down tanks about 200 yards to our left flank. Shrapnel pretty close. Went back to Ity house at first light. Put on pork for dinner with cabbage, apples and spuds. Mr

Miller frying pork chops. Should be good. We will probably have to advance tomorrow sometime as Canadians doing good work on our right. Three kilometres from main arterial road.

11th December... Attack off. Did picket at night and back to house in early morning. Had good feed of cold pork, cabbage and marrow. Slept a bit in afternoon. Things fairly quiet. Did picket from 9 to 10 when barrage was put down for 1 hour, to make Gerry jittery and reply with his guns. On picket again from 3.40 to 4.10am. Raining like blazes, Number 10 company took up our old positions.

12th December... Had breakfast and slept till 9am. Issue of chocolate, cigarettes and biscuits. Cold pork for dinner. Had to go on fighting patrol last night.

I had Jack Wyllie's **TOMMY GUN** .... and 4 mags, also spare mag for Dave's bren.

MY FIRST PATROL.

Dave Parr, Shorty Galbraith, Bill Goodall, Del Fea, Les Wylie, Fred Alderton and I. Found Ack Ack post about 300 yards south of demolitions. Gerry gear lying everywhere. Four of our tanks knocked out on the way to village of Orsogna. Bill Goodall shot up a Gerry. Thought he was alive but turned out to be very dead. Wrote to Eric Winders. Had coffee and milk and biscuits for supper.
Was Dave's (Bren) guard on patrol.

> (Patrolling (moving about, guarding, as distinct from picketing when one stood or sat in slitty or at a fixed location and guarded) was usually a three man team ... and an unpleasant cold task, for it had to be carried out at night and generally along a route covered by enemy gunners.) (O)

13th December... Wrote to Lin, fairly big letter. Shells from Gerry landing just outside. Lots of duds, but some not so "duddish". Dinner of M & V, cabbage, tatees and marrow.

14th December... **<u>MY FIRST INJURY BY SHRAPNEL</u>.**
At 11.30am I got hit on bridge of nose by shrapnel, made it bleed terrifically. Bill Goodall bandaged it. Mr Tutty got hit on head by same mortar and died at 12.30pm. Buried him same night. Very sorry to lose him. I went and got Doc to look at wound. Came back to platoon at last light. Nearly got hit again by mortar. Was let off picket by boys on account of sore nose and terrific headache. Felt better next morning.

> (The Cambridge Dictionary advises Shrapnel is bomb-fragments or small pieces of metal, that fly at speed through the air when a bomb, or shell or similar weapon, explodes.)

15th December... Had a quiet day. Nose has swelled up under eye and pretty sore.

> (On the 15th the Battalion assaulted Cemetery Ridge, just north of Orsogna with armoured support. All objectives were taken after prolonged fighting. Nevertheless the gains were held and one of the enemies main supply routes, the Orsogna to Ortona road, was blocked.) (O)

Italian farmhouses occupied by troops on the outskirts of Castelfrentano

16th December... Did picket as usual in mortar sight, 2 to 4am and pipped all day in top story of Ity house. Saw tanks getting shelled, one got direct A.P. and was set on fire. (Sherman tank) Two attacks by Luftwaffe, one on tanks. Maoris didn't get to village to support tanks.

(Nelson did a lot of 'pipping' and this is a word I can not find an explanation for. It would seem he was alert and watching all that was going on around him, either by order or for his own desire. The only time we found the word, was to do with the noise a German Spandau machine gun made when in operation ... pip pip pip. So, Nelson must have been 'on guard' looking for flashes when gun fired and listening for the pip-pipping noise.) (BBC WW2 People's War)

17th December... On picket from 4 to 6am with Mr McEwan. Les Wylie and I cooked dinner of fish rissoles and pronounced pretty good by all. Got order to be ready to move at a quarter hours notice. Tanks went through and two got to edge of Orsogna but held up. Also D Co 26th held up by Gerry putting over heavy stuff. Also mortaring. We stood by for the best part of the afternoon, liable to have to move at any time. Didn't have to move.

18th December... Not much doing.
Mort tried out his **PIAT GUN** ------->
on an Ity house. Terrific blast but didn't hurt the house much. Did a bit of pipping as have been doing for a week or more. Poor viability.

Dinner of cabbage, spuds and bully stew. Arty was cook. Pipo took bearing from top room, reported to Major Smith on observations.
At 9pm we were withdrawn for a few days spell to Castlefrentano. Into an Ity house about a mile to the west.
Our first spell from front line.

19th December... Chas came for a while in the morning and I visited him in the afternoon. Had a good wash and change of clothes. Received a cake from Times Co, Invercargill.
Great to sleep with clothes off. First time in 5 weeks.

20th December... Had a busy day. Wrote an airgraph to Lin, Vera, Mum, Frank and Dave, also a letter to Times Co thanking them for the cake. Probably have to go back to the line tomorrow night. A terrific journey in mud and slush and up and down hills.
Not looking forward to journey with full packs up on back.

#11 PLATOON on two day spell ... dated 20 December 1943

21st December... Packed up and loaded Bren Mags and got pack tied up ready to move. Received 9 letters from Lin, Mum and Hec. Received cake from Mum, stunning.

In afternoon Mr McLean told me to go again and see the doctor about the shrapnel in my nose. Did so and was told to report to a Division Surgery for operation. Distributed my four Bren mags amongst the section and handed web gear, rifle and pick to Les Kevern S.M. Came up to Castlefrentano, tea at cookhouse and left pack and overcoat at Harry Wards, carriers, while going down to see Chas at Brigade H.Q. Reported to A.D.S. about 6pm and after medical bunked for the night on stretcher. Lovely bed and five

NELSON ... WAR CORRESPONDANT !

This article appeared in the Southland Times mid December '43.

We think it's a summary of his recent war experiences he wrote up while recovering from his nose operation, with lots of time to fill. (T)

--o0o--

NEW ZEALANDERS IN ITALY

INVERCARGILL MAN'S IMPRESSIONS

Conditions under which New Zealand troops are fighting and various aspects of life in Italy are described in a letter received from Private Nelson Price, who was formerly a rural delivery service driver on the staff of The Southland Times. After describing the conditions in camp as Christmas approaches, and the treatment extended to them by the Italians, Private Price goes on to say:—

"After a period of toughening up with route marches and manoeuvres, over difficult country, we shifted to within hearing distance of the front line artillery. On the way we saw much of the Germans' destructive work in the shape of blown-up bridges and railways and this slowed our advance considerably. It is with pride that we speak of an important bridge that was saved by one of our engineers who, with only seconds to spare, dashed in and removed what was left of the demolition fuse. The same night the Hun sent a fighting patrol to blow up the bridge, but was beaten off with heavy losses.

"We eventually arrived on foot within a mile of the river Sangro and dug in. We stayed there some days, while patrols were active. The Sangro is about the size of the Oreti and is fed from sources in the nearby Appenines on our left. The night the New Zealand Division went into action the melting snow had caused a rise in the river. We forded the river with trousers rolled knee-high and then it all began. A terrific barrage was put down and in no time we were collecting 'shell happy' Huns, who seemed only too pleased to display the white flag of surrender. At dawn we reached our objective, as all good Kiwis do, and dug in smartly, but not quite smartly enough, as Jerry opened up with Spandaus and anti-tank guns. I believe I have never scooped a hole in the ground quicker in my life. I thought at the time that this must be what is meant when people say 'dig for victory.'

STREAM OF REFUGEES

"While in that village the troops had a chance to see what war did to the civilian population. Refugees were seen streaming back to their war-torn homes in hundreds, carrying what they could on their heads. Most of the country people were without boots and wore rawhide moccasins sewn up with string. Many of them had neither boots nor socks and the mud squeezed up between their toes. Practically every inch of the country was cultivated, with the result that after a few vehicles or men had passed by sticky, slimy mud was formed. The mud clung to the men's boots and gradually curved up over the toes."

From then on progress was good, writes Private Price. The advance was slow because of various advantages the Germans had. At the time of writing the New Zealanders were hammering at the gates of Orsogna.

"We have found the Italian country people hysterically pleased to welcome us," continued Private Price. "In the first village we came to, half a dozen of us stopped to fill our water bottles and in no time the total populace of about 30 was grouped round us, smiling and laughing. They gave us freshly-cooked brown bread, home-made cheese and wine."

blankets. Poor wee kiddie came in to have wounds dressed. One hand blown off by bomb and the other nearly all missing. Poor Ity woman came with husband who was shot in stomach five days ago. He died three hours after admission. Wife moaned and nearly went dotty. I nearly fell over Ity 'stiffy' on way to lav. I had a good sleep.

22nd December... Woke up to find about a dozen Maoris lying around. Head, leg and body wounds from Gerry 88's. Got on to them in a house. 5th Brigade. A Gerry with a broken leg, was beside me all night, unknown to me. Young chap with long wavy hair. Took him away before Maoris woke up!

At Castlefrentano, 9 am had morphine injection in upper arm. Felt numb. Called to operation theatre 9.30. Walked down and got onto operating table, full of beans, not for long. Major operated. Shoved needle in top and bottom of nose for anaesthetic. Don't like local anaesthetics. Went a bit numb, then he asked for knife, then probe, then pinchers, hurt a lot, then wanted fine needle and cotton, and sewed it up again. 6 double stitches. Felt pretty rotten. Doc gave me small bit of mortar shrapnel he took out. Said there may be more there and a bit of broken bone left in. He said he had lots more bigger bits I could have! Covered face with iodine. He left bottom of incision open for bleeding purposes. Came back and lay on stretcher, done out.

Then Chas came and had a yarn. Dinner of fish rissoles, great, and soup. Syd Campbell came at 3pm with 5 airgraphs, 3 from Lin and one from Mum and Alex Munro. Beautiful. Had crook headache all day. Took 4 aspros, not much better. Eye swelled up and itching, pretty sore. Doc gave me shrapnel which I showed Chas and Syd. Very small. Doc had to cut two optical nerves to get shrapnel out. Going to sleep early tonight.

23rd December... Got marching ticket this morning.

Made my way to company cookhouse. Ate there and slept the night. Dave Parr arrived 11pm crook. Stayed too.

24th December... Day of big attack. Fairly successful.
Big barrage from 4 to 7am. Couldn't sleep. Was bought back to B Ech by Mr Kerr, also Dave Parr, Jim and two others came. Slept in bivvy that night.

25th December... Xmas Day. Dinner of mashed tatees, roast pork and peas, plum pudding and sauce. Issue of patriotic parcel after tea, pretty good, also 100 tailor-made Player Cigs.

26th December... Hitch hiked to Castlefrentano to get stitches out of nose. Six in all. Bit sore. Hitch hiked back again to B Ech. Wrote to Lin at night, 20 pages.

27th December... Bad day. Wrote to Mum and Hec Thomas. Shifted in afternoon to "Shifty" Nigle's boudoir. A double bivvy. Have stretcher to sleep on tonight. Nose still pretty acky. Seems to be still a lump there. Might be bone displaced. Reinforcements coming in tonight from the south. Reinforcements didn't arrive.

28th December... Went to ADS (99) and had wound lanced. Had ached, throbbed and swelled up during the night. Looked like going septic. Doc bathed it in hot water and painted it with iodine.
Pretty sore. Lay in bivvy and read, played patience and yarned with "Shifty" the Canteen boss. Had touch of dysentery. Awfully cold day. Snowing on mountains.

29th December... Much better day today, warmer. Am getting wound bathed twice daily at R & P. Seems to be clearing up OK. Jack Wylie went out today to Oc2 Sandhurst, England. Is flying there and will be in England tomorrow night.

Dave Parr away to M.D.S. Found Major Smith yesterday morning, bullet through back of head and leg wounds. McNulty and Devlin killed. Stan Service in hospital with stomach wound. Del Fea has back wound. Doug Paul killed by airburator (mortar). **Sgt Dave Welsh** (photo) was lucky, had wireless set smashed ... was not in slitty at the time.
Four Spandaus (bracketed) opened up on them, got one of them in house.
Boys pretty shaken up. Got to objective but had to retire as rest didn't come up in time.

Sgt. D. C. Welsh, of Ohai, awarded the D.C.M.

30th December... Stayed close to bivvy. Read and slept. Davy Wilson and Shifty Kyle had to go to Castlefrentano with Canteen.

31st December... Quiet day. Read. Wrote to Mum, Marlene and Trevor. Snowed at night.

(**NEW YEARS EVE.** The weather, which had been sometimes wet and always cold for the past week and overcast and threatening on New Year's Eve, broke in the last two or three hours of 1943. A blizzard blew out of the mountains to lay one of the heaviest snow-falls within living memory as a boundary between the old year and the new. On New Year's morning snow lay about a foot deep, with drifts up to four feet deep in places.) (I)

PHOTO page 73 ...
(New Zealanders clear their bivvies' of snow on 1st January 1944. The Italians say this is the heaviest fall of snow in living memory.) (General Officer Commanding Diary)

(Alexander Turnbull Library: DA-04987-F)

1944

1st January… Day dawned. Snow everywhere. Bivvy fell on top of me. Stranded. Shifted a tarpaulin over respirators, packs and other gear. Propped it up with bivvy poles and had primus. Dried out pants and sock and boots. Slept well on stretcher.

2nd January… Snow frozen solid. Good walking. Trucks bogged. 6th Brigade coming out today. RMT away for them. Wrote to Lin, 11 pages so far.

3rd January… Read and mucked around mostly all day. Drank Xmas beer with Bill Spence from Invercargill, Bill Thayer of Gore and Bill Graham from Waianawa. Up to front at night.

4th January… Fixed handle of mug with number 10 wire. Wrote to Mum and read. Collected 1 pound pay. Saw Jim Wakefield who found a Gerry mirror and razor. Froze.

(Blizzard conditions at nights 4, 5, 6 January.) (I)

5th January... Quiet day. Mr Kerr came and enquired about my health. Said I was OK. Pretty cold all day. Lay in bed and read.

6th January... Was in bed when truck called for Bill Graham, Bill Thayter and I. Packed up in hurry and was taken by truck to Castle-frentano village. Itys working on snowdrifts on road. Snowing most all day. Taken to Ity house and joined rest of boys. Still snowing. Got Truth parcel and 2 airgraphs and telegram from Lin and airgraph from Mrs Thomas. Wrote to Lin and Mum, airgraphs. Read at night by fire. Gerry had put shell through house and killed Mrs Ity and 2 kiddies. Husband alive, with big beard... habit to not shave while bereavement in family. Pretty draughty old house.

7th January... Put in day sitting at fire. Got airgraphs from Lin, Mum and Vera. Cold day. Snow thick on ground. Put 4 pound in Pay Book, from Mum.

8th January... Got letter from Lin. Got spade from QM. Tried out Bren and Tommy. Cleaned them. Made oyster patties. Wrote to Lin at night. May be going back 'in' to take over 14th on Monday night.

> (8 January at Waikiwi, Invercargill. Lillian was at her mother's on this date. She received a Telegraph from NZ Minister for Defence Jones... saying Nelson has been reported wounded. (?) She must have known he had recovered from his 14 Dec 1943 nose injury. Wounded again ... not according to his dairy. Govt very late giving advice!)

9th January... Shaved. Church service in Ity house 9.30am. Refilled Bren mags. Watched Ity trying to bargain over purchase of bullock. Owner was offered 22 pound 10 shillings but would not sell. Equivalent of 8000 lira. Jim Gemmel re-joined platoon after over a month out. Wrote to Rev Graham.

10th January... Packed up and prepared to go up to the front line, to take over from 5th Brigade. At dinner time was told to 'stand by' and later were told we were not going in for at least two days. Great news. Possibility of being withdrawn for a month, and Poles or Indians taking over from us. Our company transport coming up soon and drivers have instructions to have lights fixed. Sounds like a move back to some base. Went on route march this afternoon to keep fit. Getting lazy without any strenuous exercise.

> (About mid-January the 2 NZ Division and 4 Indian Division, considered to be the most experienced 8th Army divisions, were ordered from the Adriatic front to the western side of Italy. They were destined for Monte Cassino, where two American Divisions were battering at German fortifications. Later the 78th British Division joined them and under General Freyberg they were a fully motorised unit, well trained and with 170 tanks.) (W)
>
> (The Second NZ was withdrawn from the stalled front line and transferred to the Cassino sector, where other allied troops were bogged down in costly fighting for a position on Monte Cassino.) (Wikipedia)

11th January... Got two parcels from Lin today, number 1 & 2. Have got up to number 3 now and one from Mum, Vera and the Times Co. Got Bren box and pannias from B Ech (B company Echelon) and packed mags away after oiling. Also put Bren away and Dave Parr's rifle. We're section for duty and made morning tea and dinner. Gordon Maze and Kelly from 12 platoon visited for nattering session. Wrote airgraph to Lin thanking her for lovely parcels. Got bivvy.

12th January... Fairly quiet day. Our air-force about, a dozen spitties at a time, dive bombed Orsogna and creek areas. Vapour trails high up. One long tail. Very pretty. Bill Goodall re-joined the platoon. Bill Stevenson put into 3 platoon. Mr Ewan, number 3 corporal to leave tomorrow for Egypt. Yarn about war being over fairly soon in Europe. Then perhaps the Japs will come in for some attention from us. Hope I can set foot on NZ soil, will stay there.

(On 12 Jan '44 Lillian received Telegram from Jones saying Nelson had been discharged from hospital ......
Somewhat late again. Lillian back at Wilton St. T)

13th January... Did very little, just loafed around. Wrote airgraph to Lin and sent her 8th Army News.

14th January... Prepared for leaving for region of Foggia. Packed up Bren box, panniers etc, also bivvies, blankets, etc. Trucks arrived 4pm, had early tea and then packed trucks. Lot of gear, including ammo. Put in 'slow' evening, had tomato soup and toast for supper. Are to leave at 11pm. Whole Division moving back.

Transport in heavy snow

LONG LINE OF TRUCKS IN SNOW AT CASTLEFRENTANO

(Casualties of the 2nd NZ Div at Sangro = 419 killed, 1243 wounded, and took 88 prisoners, from 15 Nov 1943 to 5 Jan 1944. A.T. Lib)

15th January… LEFT CASTLEFRENTANO 11pm, 14th.
Travelled 40 mile, brewed up. Half slept until daylight. Had breakfast and went 60 mile through Termoli to San Severo. Bivvied down with Jim McIntosh, 20 mile beyond town. Flat country. Hailed at night.

16th January… Got the dope from Mr McLean. We are going north of Naples, to take part on the USA 5th Army front. Probably to capture Rome. Today we go right across Italy, through Lucera, Ariano, Grottaminarda, Avellino, Baiano, Cancello and Caserta. Left bivvy area at 7am. 16 miles today. Pretty cold in trucks.

17th January… Travelled all day up to 6am. Truck broke down and Bert Grimwood and I travelled up with number 10 platoon. Stopped for night at Ity house and cleaned out a room. Very dirty place, shoved (rubbish) into corners. After cleaning out room, I poured petrol over it and lit same. Woof. The whole room was ablaze. Door blew shut with blast. Scorched spiders and fleas.!

18th January… 50 miles today. Finished journey.

> (The book **'26 BATTALION'** by Frazer D Norton … which was presented to Nelson at the completion of the War … advises on page 336….
> *"Another early start was made next morning 17th January and by 11am the battalion had reached its destination, a camp site in the valley of the Volturno River. Close by were two villages, Alife and Raviscanina. The troops debussed and moved into company areas where they erected their bivouacs amongst the olive trees. Here they remained until 5th February.")* (O)

Yesterday passed Mount Vesuvius which was active and at night saw glow from it. Plenty of Yanks around here. Had a yarn to some. Gave us a packet of smokes each. Got 3 tins from them for washing. Yesterday Maoris turned tank guns on Gerry. Took lots of prisoners. Yanks took Cassino (village) but lost half of one division.

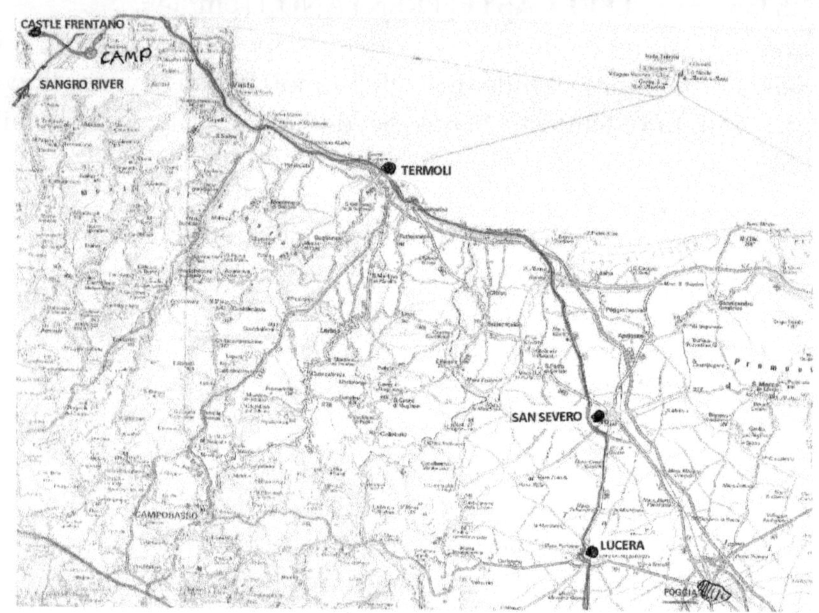

MAP 1: Travelled 4 days from east coast to west coast.
MAP 2: Continuation of 4 day trip in Italy.

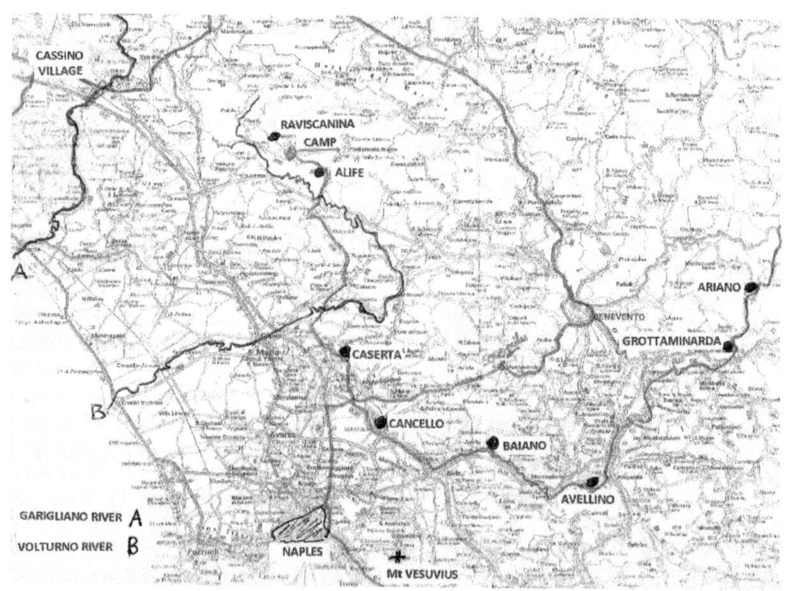

Bivvies in Company lines on the banks of the Volturno

(17th January... The New Zealanders role in the Fifth Army front had already been decided, and as they were not required until early February they were given from this date specialised training. Emphasis was laid on quick debussing from vehicles and assaults by small parties on strongpoints ... houses or fortified posts, and detailed instruction on the best methods of detecting and lifting mines, etc. (O)
(The tanks of the Division, strengthened by 52 taken over from 5 Corps reserve, were meanwhile transported by train from Vastro to Caserta, thence driven to their destination. (I)

19th January... Cleaned Bren and went for one hour route march. In afternoon went on frugal, embus and debussing practice. Had a strenuous time. Landed up in village and French Algerian troops turned on coffee. Some of boys got vino and oranges. At night I went in jeep with Jim Gemmel, who has transferred to carriers. Bill Guinn Lt was transferred to carriers yesterday. I put in an application for transfer to carriers with Bill Guinn. Will know in two days time. Then went to location of sigs and had a yarn to Charlie. Came home in dark and got a bit lost amongst the grape vines. Lft Bruce Peterson who was transferred to C Company yesterday paid us a visit. Mr Lang promoted and transferred to DC of D Company.

20th January… Went on route march to old Roman castle built 500 years ago. Very dilapidated. Had group photo taken. On return saw Shrine and Crypts. In afternoon saw yanks trying out gats. Had a yarn and showed them my bren and sniper's rifle. They took Ghandi and I over to their lines to the armoury and showed us their semiautomatic rifle, the Gerard, also the para-troop's 5 lb rifle. Pretty nice gat. At night wrote airgraph to Lin and Mum. Went for short route march and fired 10 tracer each at target. One tracer set a fire going amongst some trees on hill. All hands ran to put it out.

I got washing ready to wash and 2 Ity women said they would wash it for some soap, so I readily agreed, boiled some water and sat down and watched them wash it. Great. Gave them stick of chocolate each and box of matches. Aired blankets and washed collar of jacket. Some went for shower. Showed Ity kids how to kick football.

21st January… Went on route march to Ailano, about 3 mile to the west. Very dirty show. Lazed around in afternoon. Played poker at night.

22nd January… Went on shooting practice. Fired 100 rounds through bren. Saw boys fire off 2 mortar shells. Stalked a hare.

23rd January… Church parade in morning. Practised brigade drill in afternoon, in preparation for review by 'tiny' Freyberg tomorrow, Monday. Lot of huey. Wrote airgraph to Lin & Mum. Dave Parr came back with 600 other reinforcements for Div. Back in No.3 Section. Big attack going in on 5th Army front tonight. Landing made up coast 18 mile from Rome by 3 Yank Divs and Highlanders.

24th January... Went on parade 9am and company marched down to Brigade area. Fine spectacle of march-past. Three presentations by Freyberg ... a Military Cross & 2 Military Medals. Tiny looked fit and well. "Blood & Guts". Went to watch 11 and 12 platoons play football. (draw 3 all)

25th January... Mines lecture in morning. Parcels arrived in afternoon.

26th January... Another mines lecture in morning. Started to rain. Came home. Wrote to Lin in afternoon and airgraph to Lin & Mum at night. Got birthday cake parcel from Lin, also tissues , PK etc.

27th January... Mines lecture in morning .. had yarn to Lft Edmuston ... route march afterwards. Boys went to football in afternoon. I felt crook, headache etc. Have to go on manoeuvres tonight ... quarter to six. Not looking forward to it much.

Got airgraph from Lin and Mum today. Also a letter from Lin and 2 from Mum and letter from Times Co about sending money. Section Patrol with Bill Goodall, Bert Davidson, Keith Campbell and Bill Stevenson. 1500 yards to house on hill. Had half bottle of beer with Dan Aston afterwards.

28th January... Tried Piat out on house. Two shots. Basil Williams got hunk of shrapnel in arm. Away to hospital. Went to village to see demonstration of street fighting. Pretty feeble. In afternoon boiled billy for boys. Nice day. Lots of bombers and fighters passing overhead. Saw 103 a few days ago... all in one heap.

29th January... Went down to Volturno River and practised crossing river in boats. 5 minutes per platoon. Pretty tough marching in heat.

30th January... Wrote to Lin and Olive Holloway (Charles' wife) Received No.4 parcel from Lin. Went for walk with Dan Aston. Ity's shouted vino.

31st January... Went on hill climbing stunt. Very steep hills. Did 3 frugal attacks per section. Div Cav shooting up gulley. Bullets whining everywhere. Cleaned up bren in afternoon. Rumour of a move tomorrow night. Made application for transfer to HQ 26 Battalion for position as Driver to Battalion, through Lt Harvey.

1st February... Took brens down to armoury and had them greased. Both barrels shooting dead in. Boys played 12 platoon. Beaten 5 to 3. No word about shifting tonight yet. Got 18 bren mags filled ... 25 in each mag. Have to carry 1000 rounds for each bren. Think I've missed on the Driver's job.

2nd February... Wrote airgraph to Lin & Mum. Shot 5 rounds through Gerry Spandau today. Great gun. I like it miles ahead of our bren for accuracy. Pretty heavy. B Co 26 played B Co 23 football today. No word of shift yet.

3rd February... Route march in morning to village Ailano and dig attack on way back. I was CO of section !!! In afternoon went down to Volturno to watch bridging of river and anti-tank and jeep crossing. At night had big vino party... 40 present. Bed 11.30pm.

4th February... Route march to near village and up hill. Very hard on wind. Sweated a lot. Cup of tea at 10am. Wrote to Lin. 'Needles' on the go. May shift Sunday. At night played poker with Dan Aston, Keith Campbell and Josh Holloway. Lost 30 Lira.

5th February... Busy packing up for shift supposed to be coming off tonight. Up about 40 mile to within 2 mile of Gerries F.D. Will be in range of big guns, but not under direct observation. Laurie Clarke, Dan Aston and Bill Stevenson left out of battle. Shared out bren mags. Very high wind blowing. Moved up to Guadolia and arrived 2am. Made three trips to road for gear. Carried bren down bank and dug in, got straw from old house and had two hours sleep.

6th February... Breakfast, Gerry shelling road about 40 yards away. Hot morning. Boys cleaned out room in Ity house and Jim Mc, Les Wylie and I went over creek for firewood.

****** **<u>I STOOD ON GERRY SCHU-MINE</u>.** Wicked things. Blew foot off and had my face lifted. Broken jaw and felt pretty crook. Two American gunners were on the scene in about 10 minutes. Made me lay flat and injected 2 shots of morphine in leg. Got stretcher and carried me about 100 yards to ambulance. Tourniquet on leg 20 minutes by arrival at 18 Field Ambulance Centre. Was chloroformed and I woke up in British 14 Casualty Clearing Station. Got transfusions, and my jaw set and wired, and they applied leg dressing.

A NEW TYPE OF NAZI MINE; IT CONSISTS OF A WOODEN BOX, IN WHICH IS PLACED A HALF-POUND BLOCK OF TNT.

The Nazi practice of laying [illegible] to impede Allied advances in Italy is well known, and among the various types of mines used is the wooden box-mine shown above. In it is placed ½-lb. of TNT., and a detonator is passed through a hole in the front of the box. The lid is prevented from closing properly by a small twig, which, when displaced, allows the box to close, thus knocking out the pin and firing the detonator.

The **Schu-mine 42** was a German anti-personnel blast land-mine used during the Second World War. It consisted of a simple wooden box with a hinged lid containing a 200 g block of cast TNT. A slot in the lid pressed down on the striker retaining pin. Sufficient pressure on the lid caused the pin to move, releasing the striker which triggered the detonator. The mine was cheap to produce, and its wooden body made it more difficult to detect with early metal detectors.

(Wikipedia WW2 Schu-mine)

The BOOK "Official Record *26 Battalion*" page 340, records ...

~~parties had repaired the track leading in to it.~~ During the day one man from 11 Platoon trod on a Schu mine and lost part of his foot. Like many others he sought to line his trench with hay, but unfortunately for him the Germans had mined the area; it was later taped off by the Provost section.

PAGE 340 – 6 FEB 1944: OFFICIAL HISTORY 26 BATTALION NZ WW2:

> (The reason Nelson was near the **Garigliano River** and stood on the mine is really unclear. His dairy says he was gathering firewood. Above he was gathering straw for his bed and he told son Trevor ... he wanted to relieve himself, then saw two destroyed German tanks and wandered over, to look at them. (Later he named his dog **'Gary'**)

(Whatever the reason, he was later able to return to his family.)

7th February... Shifted to 2NZGH in morning, eyes pretty dim. Was there 2 days... so I was told later and then was shifted by ambulance to British Hospital No. 65 at Naples. Arrived at Ward 1 and Sister McKinnon stayed and saw me comfortable.

> (9th February Airgraph sent to Lillian from K G Hall Assistant Matron 2 GH ... *"I'm so sorry your husband has been posted dangerously ill. He came to our hospital 2 days ago, minus his right foot and some shrapnel in his other leg, his jaw has been fractured and both eyes injured ... though Doctor says he will not loose his sight. Though his condition is grave there is every hope he will soon be on the up-grade. He is being attended by specialists and I can assure you that everything possible is being done for him. I do hope I can give you a more favourable report next week."*

The FOLLOWING WEEKS: I was in Ward 1 for a week. Had Sister Macdonald and Captain Grieve 2GH come to see me. They brought airgraphs on next trip about fortnight later.

Had visit from 2GH Padre who bought me a pen and mirror and also gave me a comb. Wouldn't take any money for them.
Was shifted to Ward 7 and was there 2 months. Had South African orderlies… Gitbert, David, Jobo and Jacob. Got up after 1 month and went around in wheelchair and graduated to crutches.
Cosmopolitan population in hospital … wounded Germans, British, French, Gurkhas (Indians), South Africans and Kiwis. Sisters Smith and Griffiths very efficient, but far too much work to do.
Assistant Matron (ex Aussie) was very nice. Put in a pretty evil four weeks getting the jaw to set. Leg pretty sore.
Lofty and Smithy (Grenadiers) great scouts. George Shadbolt and I got around fairly often. George is still with me and has a homer too.
Left 65th British Hospital on Easter Monday.

(The Army is quite considerate and does not allow wounded men to fight ... they have to been 100% fit and in full awareness of where and why they are there. They are then able to act and provide as much safety for themselves and their Army mates. Nelson had many days off fighting due to his nose wound and was not allowed back until it had reasonably healed and caused no pain. Nelson's 'homer' wound (lost foot) means he will not be going back to the front to fight, but will be sent home… his war was over. T)

(17 February… Sister Macdonald sent Telegram to In'gill with Nelson's injury details … days later Lillian received a Telegram from Minister Jones dated 19 Feb saying … *"Much regret to inform you that your husband has been reported wounded and dangerously ill. Diagnosis amputation right foot, compound fracture mandible and multiple wounds (stop) The Prime Minister desires me to convey to you on behalf of the government his sincere wishes for a speedy recovery. F Jones.)*

(23 February… Another Telegram from Mr Jones to Lillian *"Pleased to inform that further cable reports your husband has* *been removed from both the Dangerously and Seriously ill lists.")*

Write the address in large BLOCK letters in the panel below.
The address must NOT be typewritten.

TO:– MRS N. PRICE.
77 WILTON ST.,
INVERCARGILL
NEW ZEALAND

22 FEB 1944

Write the message very plainly below this line.

Sender's Address 60171 – Sister M J Macdonald. 2 N.Z.G.H. C.M.F.

17. 2. 44.

Dear Mrs Price, I am writing this to let you know that your husband is improving. He was transferred to a British Hospital just temporarily, so, yesterday, his Medical Officer and I went in to see him.

His main worry was that at this particular place, he had been unable to procure an air-graph form on which to write you, so, I promised to write this for him & also to send him some forms.

He also asked me to send you a cable which went this morning.

We hope to have him back with us shortly, but in the meantime, someone always manages to go in & see him.

With kind regards.

Yours sincerely

J. Macdonald

This space should not be used.

MAKE SURE THAT THE ADDRESS IS WRITTEN IN LARGE BLOCK LETTERS IN THE PANEL ABOVE

17 February 1944... Airgraph from Sister M J Macdonald to Lillian.

(Most of February and all of March dates are blank and the dairy resumes on April 9. T)

LADY FREYBERG:

While at 'Hospital 65', Lady Freyberg, wife of General Bernard Freyberg (commander of 2 NZ Division) came and had about a quarter hour yarn with me. Nice old girl. I had been to theatre and had face fairly plastered with bandages after inlaying operation.

General Bernard Freyberg and his wife at Wellington 15 June 1946.

The book .....

"GENERAL LORD FREYBERG VC" by Peter Singleton-Gates has comments of this visit too ... on page 274 ...

Quote... "Lady Freyberg, with her ability for overcoming obstacles, had left Bari and was in Naples visiting New Zealanders in hospital there. The author is indebted to Nelson Price of Invercargill for this endearing personal remembrance of the General's wife..........

"I had just returned from surgery and was still under the influence of the drug pentothal, which affects me after an operation as if I were intoxicated. Matron, a sister and a visitor arrived at my cot and I understood Matron to say 'This is Lady Freyberg to see you Private Price', to which I suitably replied in a daze: "How do you do?" ... then, something seemed to click in my befuddled brain, and I burst out with "Are you Tiny's wife?" to which my visitor with a huge smile, said "Of course I am. Why not?"

It did me the world of good. "We admired him (Freyberg) for his courage, from which we drew our inspired fighting ability, or should I say, refusal to allow our fear to show too obviously." .... end quote. (G)

9th April... Arrived at 2GH Caserta by ambulance. Put in Ward H Room 4 and got George beside me. Stayed 2 days. Had Keith Campbell, Dan Aston and Ken Harvey in to see me. Went by wheelchair to see Del Fea. Looked pretty crook. Del at 2GH going home.

(The first NZ Army attack at Cassino was on the 17th February where all Battalions were involved. (24, 25, 26, & 28 Maori) They fought their way into Cassino town mid-March and in early April the NZ Division was withdrawn from the Cassino area with 343 deaths and over 600 wounded.) (N)

The JOURNEY BACK TO NZ.

12th April... Left 2GH by ambulance. Put on train at 4pm. Train didn't leave 'till 7pm. One hell of a trip. I was on the top of a tier of three sprung stretchers. Nearly bounced out of bed often. Got 'fanny adam' sleep. Bacon and bread for breakfast on train. Came through Foggia and eventually arrived at Bari.

13th April... Reached Bari at 10.30am. Taken at 1pm to Ward 13 Room C (3 GH NZ) and found George Shadbolt in same room. Very pleased. All jaw cases in same room. Doc Dunn good chap. Had reboarding papers made out last week. Received 12 parcels from home, also lots of mail and airgraphs. Have been writing regularly. Lin and kids OK. Dying to get home. Heard boat may be leaving next Thursday. Chas may get yet.

(**26 April** Telegram from F Jones to Lillian states ....
"Further cable reports amended diagnoses. Your husband multiple bomb wounds. (1) Right foot amputation through lower third leg. (2) Penetrating face with compound fracture mandible. (3) penetrating left hand. (4) penetrating left arm. (5) penetrating anterior Chest Wall. (6) Tattooing face, neck, and chest right. (stop) He was removed from both the dangerously and seriously ill lists as previously advised. F Jones."

29th April... Just got a note from Chas ... Ward 4 Room D and going to see him after tea. He may get home on same boat.
Have had a roomful of chaps to see me nearly every day during the last fortnight. But Mart Donnelly, Lft Alf McClean, Joe Richardson, Bill Goodall, Orb and Ghandi (Fred Alderton)... all passed on, in Cassino battle. Pretty awful show. Nearly cleaned up my platoon.

Ray Sutherland, Sid Rogers and Sammy Kennard ex Waianawa, in to see me today. Ray looking well. Sid is a patient (rupture) Buried Bill Stevenson yesterday. Great chap and a wonderful singer.

30th April... Dentist examines jaw in morning. Wrote airgraphs to Lin, Mum, Dave and Jim Fisher. Went to see Chas in afternoon and had a long yarn. Dave Welsh and Lindsay Edgar came to see me. Met Sister Winnie Bell from Makarewa. Alf McLean told me to look her up and make myself known. Told her Alf was killed 30/3/44. She was very cut up. Cheered her by showing snaps of Lin and kiddies after learning she went to Tech with Lin. Feeling grand but tired after trip over to see Chas.

1st May... Doctor says I am to go to theatre tomorrow to have wire removed from jawbone as end of wire sticking through gum into mouth. Also infection setting in on cheek. Will go and see Chas today. Dave Welsh coming in on Wednesday. Doctor Dunn.

2nd May... Theatre cancelled until tomorrow Wednesday. Doc says will not prevent me catching hospital ship. Saw Chas yesterday. Looking well. He had pay-books collected so appears as if he is going home on same boat.

3rd May... Waiting on boat. Got kit.

4th May... Sewed on 23 buttons on B D. (= Battle Dress) Great excitement.

2nd May 1944... Lillian receives welcome news.

NELSON TO RETURN TO NEW ZEALAND

N.Z. MILITARY FORCES, BASE RECORDS,
P.O. BOX 3044,
WELLINGTON.
2nd May, 1944.

Ref. No.
471269

Mrs.L.E.Price,
77 Wilton St.,
INVERCARGILL.

Dear Mrs. Price,

Advice has been received that 471269 Pte. N. Price, will be returning to New Zealand. At present I cannot undertake to inform you of the actual date of his arrival because the transport arrangements are not known to this office; however, if there is any opportunity of giving you further advice in this connection, prior to his arrival, you may depend that this will be done.

Meantime you should use his usual address for any mail.

Yours faithfully,

Director.

B.R.197C.

5th May... **THE DAY:**

Got up early and shaved, had breakfast and dressed in B D. Feels grand. Minutes go pretty slow. Going as "sitting patient".

9.30am and no sign of leaving yet. Going by ambulance to Taranto. Gerry plane overhead at 6am. Vapour trail. Very high. Ack Ack opened up. White smoke bursts. Sister Bell came in and shook hands. Promised to visit her parents at 26 Beatrice St. Travelled to Taranto. Was lucky to get a front seat. Came by Casamassima and Gioia. 80 mile. Arrived on wharf. About 100 ambulances lined up.

Got papers of injuries from Doc. They read……

(Diagnosis) BC, BW, MULT, FOOT WITH AMPUTATION THROUGH LOWER ONE THIRD LEG. FACE PEN WITH FRACT, COMP MANDABLE HAND (L) ANTERIOR CHEST WALL PEN. FACE, CHEST CORNEAL, ABRAS, 3 GH Bari. Signed … R & L.

Nelson sent this telegram 5 May .. (but it is date-stamped 15 May) to Lillian, obviously happy to be headed home to her and NZ.

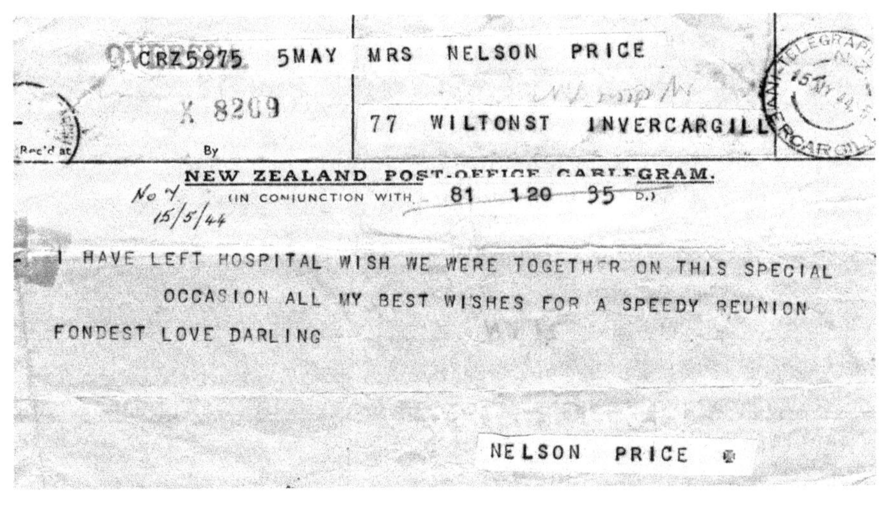

CRZ5975 5MAY MRS NELSON PRICE

X 8209

77 WILTONST INVERCARGILL

Rec'd at

By

NEW ZEALAND POST-OFFICE CABLEGRAM.

No 4 (IN CONJUNCTION WITH 81 120 35 D.)

15/5/44

I HAVE LEFT HOSPITAL WISH WE WERE TOGETHER ON THIS SPECIAL OCCASION ALL MY BEST WISHES FOR A SPEEDY REUNION FONDEST LOVE DARLING

NELSON PRICE

The SS "WANGANELLA"

The ship just pulling in to berth. She looked grand. Three red crosses along her side, ship painted white. Waited from 1 pm to 5 before our ambulance was backed in. Went up gangplank under own steam and to B Deck. Lovely cots, each with reading light, soft mattresses, spotless sheets and ash trays. Had tea of tatties and white gravy and what I think was rabbit. Slept intermittently and had a bit of headache.

6th May... Poached egg and toast for breakfast. Washed and received two airgraphs from Lin and 1 from Mum. Lin's airgraphs told about receiving 303 and Lft Grieve, also of her & Olive and Mrs McInevney working the Oracle. Chas on same ship etc. Found Chas' bunk last night and dying to see him to talk about Oracle.

(Do not understand this bit about the Oracle... T)

Pretty good attention. Went on deck last night and saw the last of colourful but rotten Italy. Went to pictures on Port Deck. Not Bad. Passed the time. Saw Chas this afternoon.

7th May… Up 8am. Abscess on cheek not going down yet. Got bit of sticking plaster. Smell of leg in plaster pretty putrid at times in Ward. Fog last night. Fog horn blown every minute. Kept us awake a fair bit. Speed in fog reduced to half. Had tea at the table for 'sitting' patients. Was grand. First time I had sat at a table for months. Del Fea got up too. He's doing fine. Comes from Winton.

8th May… Up early. Yarned. Washed and had breakfast of 1 egg and sausage. Had 2 eggs originally (light diet) but swapped chap 1 egg for his sausage. Might have bacon and egg tomorrow. Went up on deck for fresh air and stroll around. Bought toffee and razor at canteen… no blades. Doc had inspection at 11am for scabies and lice etc. George couldn't put out tongue as teeth wired. Have to hang around in afternoon and wait on dentist. Might get my teeth yet. Hope so. Very much can't stand light diet.

9th May… Turned down for teeth. No hope until I get dental gum grafted. Disappointed. Started through Suez canal at 7am. After breakfast went on deck and had a good look all morning. Canal

guarded by Wog soldiers with Ack Ack (photo) and Boffers. Balloon barrages. Took all day to go through Canal. Wonderful piece of work. 90 mile long. 90 yards wide and 90 feet deep. Took 30 years to build. Sunken ships in parts of Canal. Arrived at the Port of Suez near dark and anchored in the bay besides dozens of war ships, cargo boats and oil tankers. Sat on deck till dark. Stop exasperating. Dying to get home.

10th May... Tuesday. Shifted at daylight and pulled in to port of Tufix (Tewfik) about 4 miles away from Suez. Can see the City of Suez across the bay. Harbour just packed with ships of all kinds and nationalities. Lots of Liberty ships. Yanks. Pretty hot today. Changed into shorts much too big for me. Flies very troublesome. Lots of Wog wharfies working the barges. Today unloaded about 18 stretcher cases bound for South Africa. Stretcher bearers pretty stupid. Didn't know which way to face. See Chas daily for short yarn. Can't settle down much. Getting pretty impatient. May be here 'till Friday. Sewed buttons on Battle Dress today. Intend to keep it.

11th May... Rained this morning. Remarkable. Didn't know it ever rained in Suez. Wogs unloading barges of flour slipping on planks. Falling back into barges. Funny. Received airgraphs from Lin, Mum, Mrs Thomas, Aunty Jess, Eric Winders at Times Co. Pretty good.

Lin very pleased about jaw knitted up. Must see Chas and give him the news. Changed library books. Only allowed one on account of embarkation of sick tomorrow.

12th May... Friday. In morning took on board 180 A.P.Rs. from Helwin Hospital and Maadi 2nd half of 11th reinforcement. They arrived Maadi 2 days ago, about 2000. At noon during dinner the ropes were untied and we steamed out of Suez. Very glad to be on our way again after 4 days in port and not allowed to leave ship.
Four days was muck up by Army about boats arrival. Getting hotter and hotter. Sweat a lot in bed at night. Even to turnover is an effort that brings perspiration. Skipping along about 12 knots. Went down to see Chas this afternoon. Pictures last night. Saw Bruce Peterson in afternoon and he's doing well.

13th and 14th May... 'Gordam' hot. Almost unbearable. Sailing down Red Sea, should arrive Aden tomorrow. Pulled hairs out of inlay op this morning, (5) feels fine. Only three weeks from home. Whoopee ! Doing about 15 knots. Paid today.

15th, 16th, 17th May... Same thing each day. Nothing out of the ordinary.

18th May... Wednesday. Always very hot and sweat continuously. Sleep in short undies only. Are to reach Colombo, Ceylon, south of India on Friday, then 10 days to Fremantle, Perth, West Australia and then 8 days to Wellington. Leg not healed up yet.

19th and 20th May... In Indian Ocean. Still very hot. Making good time. May reach Colombo Friday. Intend writing Lin airgraph today. Chas got up for the first time, was assisted to lav and back. Felt pretty weak. Got big issue cigarettes .. double lot. 600, 8 ounce bacca and matches. All Capstan and State Express. Sea very choppy and boat rolling quite a bit.

21st May... Wrote airgraph to Lin and Mum. Being sent from Bombay. May get home before them. Chas sent Olive a cable. Same as I sent from 3GH. Leg not healed up yet. Being dressed every other day. Sisters work hard. Am still on light diet. Brains, rabbit and very old and tough chicken flesh.
Are due to arrive at Colombo in morning. Am allowed to go on leave. Only got 30 shillings. ($NZ3.00) Believe lots of presents can be bought. Collected a navy blue suit yesterday, to be worn ashore. Has light blue braid around arm for identity purposes. A bit cooler today. Lightening last night out west. Looks like rain today. See Chas daily. He's slowly improving.

Asked Doc yesterday about going to plastic surgery at Burwood, Christchurch. Seems to think it will be OK.

22nd May... Arrived Colombo 8am and sailed up harbour past dozens of ocean going ships including 2 aircraft carriers. One arrived in early afternoon. Enormous looking things. Lots of cargo boats, launches, Indians, barges etc. Just another Wog harbour, like Suez. Couldn't get leave on account of crutches. Had two goes but no luck. Got chap to do shopping for me. Bought me a pair of bookends. Elephants. Consider Lin will like 'em a lot. Moonstone necklace and elephant broach. Boys spent a lot of money. I bought a coconut from an Indian on oil barge out of porthole. Whole, for 20 cigarettes. Drank the juice and played bowls with the rest. Boys arrived back 3pm with all sorts of gear. Some had boxes of Tea. Two pounds weight cost them 4/6 (NZ 45 cents) a pound. Cigars at 10/- ($NZ 1.00) for 50, and all variety of jewellery. Sailed from Colombo round about 5pm. Sea pretty rough.

23rd May... Tuesday. Sea still heaving, got a pretty crook head ache through it. Leg not healed. Nearly back where it started. Vaseline, gauze dressing, and again sulfonamide powder. Went to pictures at night. "Raffles" Pretty poor. Have to go at 5.30pm to get a seat.

24th May… 8 days from Fremantle. Saw Chas this afternoon.
(Nothing recorded for 25, 26, 27 and 28 May)

28 May … Ship's MENU …… H.M.A.H.S. "Wanganella"
(Her, Majesties, Army, Hospital, Ship)
(White card with Red Cross behind ship (see page 95 and below)

Nelson has noted on the cover, the arrival dates and the main ports they reached, on their trip home.
Inside is the 'Luncheon Menu' for 28 May 1944 … as below ………..

As well as the Menu he has gathered signatures
of some of the men he travelled home with.

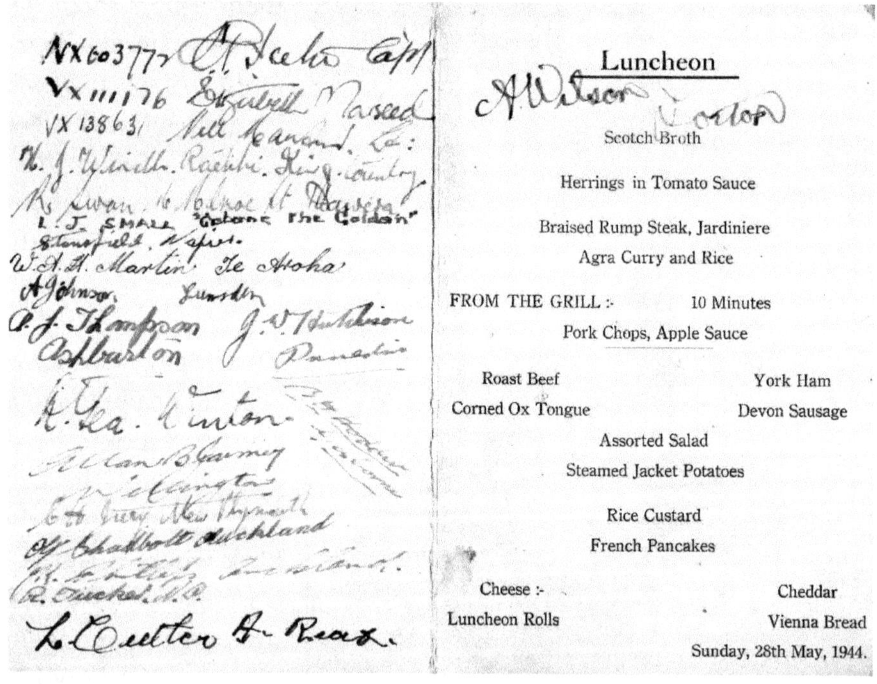

Luncheon

Scotch Broth

Herrings in Tomato Sauce

Braised Rump Steak, Jardiniere

Agra Curry and Rice

FROM THE GRILL :- 10 Minutes

Pork Chops, Apple Sauce

Roast Beef — York Ham

Corned Ox Tongue — Devon Sausage

Assorted Salad

Steamed Jacket Potatoes

Rice Custard

French Pancakes

Cheese :- — Cheddar

Luncheon Rolls — Vienna Bread

Sunday, 28th May, 1944.

29th May… Went and saw Chas this afternoon. Got a ship's menu from Chas. Weather getting pretty cold now. Chaps gradually putting more on, trousers, jackets and jerseys. Are to arrive Fremantle Thursday morning. Hoping hard to get leave.

30 May 1944... Tuesday

(Lillian must have written again to NZ Base Records, on 20 May to get details of Nelson's ship's arrival and hoping to be able to meet him at Lyttleton Port. But they are giving nothing away in their reply below dated 30 May. T)

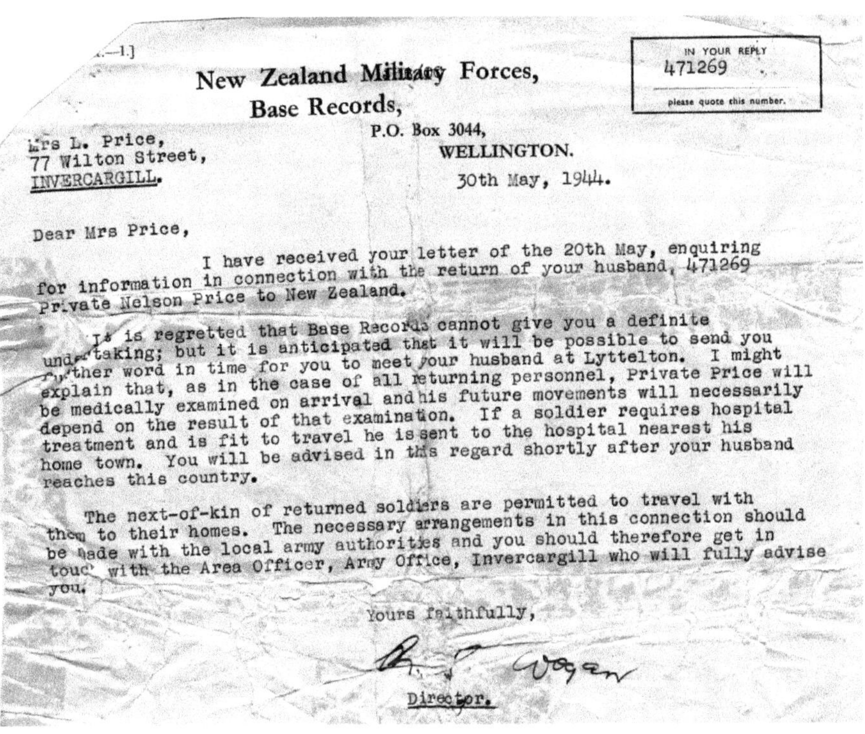

IN YOUR REPLY 471269 please quote this number.

New Zealand Military Forces,
Base Records,
P.O. Box 3044,
WELLINGTON.

Mrs L. Price,
77 Wilton Street,
INVERCARGILL.

30th May, 1944.

Dear Mrs Price,

I have received your letter of the 20th May, enquiring for information in connection with the return of your husband, 471269 Private Nelson Price to New Zealand.

It is regretted that Base Records cannot give you a definite undertaking; but it is anticipated that it will be possible to send you further word in time for you to meet your husband at Lyttelton. I might explain that, as in the case of all returning personnel, Private Price will be medically examined on arrival and his future movements will necessarily depend on the result of that examination. If a soldier requires hospital treatment and is fit to travel he is sent to the hospital nearest his home town. You will be advised in this regard shortly after your husband reaches this country.

The next-of-kin of returned soldiers are permitted to travel with them to their homes. The necessary arrangements in this connection should be made with the local army authorities and you should therefore get in touch with the Area Officer, Army Office, Invercargill who will fully advise you.

Yours faithfully,

Director.

30th May... Nearing Australia. Due to arrive Thursday morning. Weather much cooler now. Put on singlet this morning.
First time since leaving Italy. Didn't go to see Chas. Too rough.
Got paid today. Ten shillings. Can't buy much in Fremantle or Perth on that. Doc gave me his collar badge. Pretty good of him.

31st May... Due in Fremantle tomorrow. Not sure about leave.

Luncheon MENU for 31 May 1944

Luncheon

Potage, Paysanne

Schnapper and Salmon Croquettes : Provencale

Braized Rabbit and Bacon

Delhi Curry and Rice

FROM THE GRILL :- 10 Minutes

Rump Steak

Roast Beef | Roast Lamb

York Ham | Devon Sausage

Assorted Salad

Steamed Jacket Potatoes

Tapioca Custard

Bengal Fritters & Lemon Syrup

Cheese :- Cheddar

Luncheon Rolls | Vienna Bread

Wednesday, 31st May, 1944.

SISTER MACDONALD and SISTER POLLOCK, nurses on the *Wanganella* on trip home to NZ. Photo taken by a Private French.

Sister Macdonald mentioned a few times by Nelson in his diary.

1st June...

Arrived at Fremantle, main port of West Australia at 7am. Glad to see land again. Harbour full of warships and cargo ships and about 5 submarines. Yank subs and big ones. Very rusty. One just came in early this morning. Got leave OK and disembarked at 10.30am.

Red Cross cars waiting for us. Got in one with Harry and Les Small. Were driven to Perth about 11 mile away. About 40 cars. Did some shopping and got some things for Chas. Had great dinner at Red Cross place. Fruit cake, salad etc, then did the shopping. Got back to ship 3pm. Supposed to get back at 2.30pm.

Enjoyed the outing immensely. Chas very pleased with the stuff I got for him. Wood Vase (Wet hardwood), Amber necklace, "Target for tonight" was game for his son Brian. Would have liked it for Trevor, and a brooch. Due to pull out anytime tonight.

2nd June... Left Fremantle 5pm last night.
Today got paid 30 shillings (NZ$3.00) final before reaching NZ.

3rd June... Seas awfully rough and ship rolling from side to side. Too bad for getting around on crutches. Issue of 200 cigarettes today. Have arranged to get Les Small's issue too. Cost 13 shillings.
Can't sleep at night. Thinking of home and how near we are to it. Only another week. 7 days and we pull into Wellington. Trying to scrounge some black felt for making a pair of titles. Sister gave me an 'Australia' title last night and some buttons for Harry.

4th June... Issue of half bottle beer today. Weekly issue. Trying to get an Aussie Hat. Orderly trying for me. Only 6 more days to Wellington. Whacko. Longing to see NZ again. Trip going very slowly. Boat rolling still but not so badly.

5th June... Monday. Good going. Not so much rolling. Leg not healed yet. Sent telegrams to Lin and Mum and trying to get two for Trevor and Marlene. Haven't seen Chas for three days.
Issue of 1lb Ceylon Tea today (Red Cross). Sewed on Brigade titles and patches this morning. According to broadcast ROME fell today. (to Allies) 5th Army making good progress.

6th June... Four months today since I got blown up.
Opening of second front in Europe. Just listened to speech by General Eisenhower, Commander-in-Chief. Boys very excited and clustered around wireless. Passed through Bass Strait between Australia and Tasmania today. On the last lap. Only three more days left. Had yarn with Red Cross chap for about an hour ....

invasion includes spearhead to Norway, Denmark, Belgium, Holland and France.

7th June... Reports of invasion state 10,000 sorties were flown by R.A.F. over the French coast. Airborne troops captured Guernsey and Jersey Islands. No German fighters over coast. King gives speech and Churchill says things going better than expected.
My leg gradually healing up. May be right by time NZ shows up. Only 2 and a half days to go. Have been held up by one engine running a bearing. Lost some hours, otherwise would have arrived Wellington Friday night.

8th June... Thursday. One and a half days to go. No word yet if being taken on to Lyttelton. Don't think so. Gliders being used on Western front. Also landing has been made in Greece by para-troops and airborne troops. Much air activity over France. 5 Army in Italy pushing Germans back up past Rome. Russians attacking Germans in Caucasus and Romania.

10th June... Up early and then was late for breakfast. NZ in sight and what a great feeling to see it again. Saw Mt Egmont from a porthole at breakfast time. Went on deck and saw South Island (Cape Farewell) from starboard side. Going through Cook Strait. Should make Wellington by noon. Don't know yet if Wanganella is going to Lyttelton. Will probably arrive Christchurch tomorrow morning. So near and yet so far from home. Dressed in battledress with patches and titles. Boys very excited. No wonder.

Unloading began 2pm. Finished about 5pm. Ship to take us to Lyttelton. WO2 Bob Grieve called on Chas and me and told us Lin and Olive in Christchurch to meet us. Great excitement !! Due to leave here tomorrow night 5pm. Arrive Lyttelton at dawn, Monday. Only Sandy from Ashburton and I for tea tonight. Very lonely and dying to get home now.

11th June... Met Sir Cyril Newall, Governor of New Zealand, on hospital boat, also Lady Newall, and Fred Jones the Minister of Defence. Shook hands all round.
Went with Arthur Johnstone to his sister's place in Lower Hutt per Red Cross car. Had great dinner. Back to boat by 2.30pm. Sailed out of harbour at 5pm. Couldn't sleep too well. Too excited.

12th June... Monday. Entered Lyttleton harbour 6am and first persons on wharf were Lin and Olive Holloway. A truly great sight. Disembarked about 9.30am and travelled by hospital train as far as Dunedin. Met Auntie Jess, Em, Millie and Uncle Will at Christchurch, (Lillian's mother's Stevens family) and Daisy, Jessie etc, at Ashburton station. (More Stevens family) Arrived Dunedin 8pm. Slept on train. Lin & Olive stayed at boarding house.

> (I read or heard somewhere that Lillian and Olive were allowed to travel on the train with their men. T)

> (A June 13 Southland newspaper announced the expected arrival of the train at noon that day and advised ... The Train left Lyttleton yesterday morning and the Southern Military District asked for the train to be held at Dunedin overnight. This meant much more comfort for the returning men who were saved an all-night journey in wintery weather, and also allowed the more agreeable time of noon at the Invercargill Station than nearer midnight.
> The train stopped at Balclutha, Clinton, Gore and Edendale before reaching Invercargill.
> Some of the Southern men were taken to Christchurch and Dunedin Hospitals and more were taken to the Gore and Southland Hospitals. It was planned to take the walking wounded (Nelson) to their homes by the Red Cross cars, but family helped Nelson get to 77 Wilton St.

NAMES OF MEN

The names of Southland men in this draft of sick and wounded are (the address is Invercargill unless otherwise stated):—

Lieutenant B. R. Peterson, Corporal G. W. Agnew, Sergeant G. A. Boyce, Corporal I. C. Buchan (Balclutha), Corporal F. W. Cavanagh (Waikaia), Private R. D. Dobbie (Menzies Ferry, detraining Dunedin), Private L. G. Due, Private R. M. Fairbairn (Kennington), Private B. D. Fea (Winton), Private L. R. Fletcher (Otatara), Private S. D. Gilson (Clifton), Private T. A. Hall (Lawrence), Signalman C. E. Holloway, Private J. R. Horrell (Gore, detraining Dunedin), Private E. Jennings (Glenham), Private A. S. Johnson (Lumsden), Trooper R. Jones (Beaumont), Private L. J. Kreft (Milton), Private R. S. MacDonald, Private O. S. McNoe (Waitahuna, detraining Dunedin), Sergeant J. H. Mathias (Waipiata), Sapper O. J. Morham (Clinton), Sapper L. H. Ogilvie (Tuatapere), Private N. Price.

The Invercargill newspaper added a list of all the names of the returning men. Chas Holloway and Nelson included, and probably others through to Z not on our cutting.

13th June...
HOME TODAY:
1pm. Most of my relations on Invercargill's Station. Wilson Blakie drove me home per 8hp Ford. Mum and Mrs Thomas and Marlene at 77 Wilton Street. Wonderful to be home again and not in the slightest sorry to be back, believe me.

Lillian has added ... 'Trevor at School and was bought home by Wilson Blakie.'

(My recollections ... I was aged 7 then and this is probably the earliest child-hood memory I have ... of walking into our kitchen/living room and seeing my father sitting on the bay-window settee, in Army uniform, with only one shoe and crutches nearby. I do not remember running over and giving him a big welcome home hug or anything. T)

MARLENE aged 5 ... **TREVOR** aged 7

(From this point on, Nelson's Diary has notes written by himself and by Lillian. T.)

VISITORS on 13th Mrs James Price (Nelson's mother Hannah) Mr & Mrs P W Thomas (Lillian's parents) Mr & Mrs A W Blakie (Wilson and Mrs is Nelson's sister Vera) Mr & Mrs D M Price (Nelson's brother Dave) Nancy & Harold and children Kevin & Leona. (Nelson's sister Nan and his brother Harold) Athol, Valerie & Heather. (children of the Blakies) Venetia, Earl & Essex. (children of Dave). In the evening Mr Sefton Hunter (unknown to TP) and Lillian's mother (Elsie Thomas) visited.

14th June... Visitors .. Vera, Mrs Holland, Merilyn, Mrs Holloway (Olive) and Mrs Thomas. Evening Jack Graham.
Hospital in afternoon.

15th June... Sefton Hunter took me to Times Office for afternoon tea with ladies staff. Yarn with R J Gilmore Managing Director of Times. Wilson Blakie visit in afternoon. Wrote letter in evening.

16th June... Friday. Hospital in morning.
Welcome home at Times Garage by fellow drivers.
Evening visit from Mr & Mrs Dwyer and Kay.

17th June... Saturday morning... Visit from Auntie Vic and Dolly. (Vic is Victoria, Nelson's Aunt, a sister of his father Jimmy Price .. Dolly ?) Grandma Price (Hannah) came to dinner.
Dave Blair and Mrs Dalrymple for afternoon tea. Frank, Kate and Joan for tea and evening. (Frank is Nelson's brother, and Joan is F & K's daughter)

18th June... All went to Church at North In'gill, then to Blakie's for dinner and tea. Mr & Mrs Tait & family called at 77 Wilton, then at Blakies. Mrs & Mrs Fisher called at 77 and left swedes.

19th June... Monday. Hospital in morning.
P W Thomas gardening. (presume at 77. Percy is Lillian's father.)
Saw G W Gifford and got petrol licence. (was still rationed)

20th June... Tuesday. Jack McDonald visited morning. (not sure if he is a McDonald relation or not) Phil Hardy visit afternoon.
Went to Welcome-Home Chas Holloway home from hospital. Evening Mrs Brandford came and polished and stained crutches.

21st June... To hospital in Morning.
Visits from Mrs Bell (mother of Nurse Winnie Bell), Molly Henderson, Sandra & Russell, Nancy & Kevin, Kath Holland & Merilyn.
Wilson took Nel to his mother's for an hour or so. He saw Vera, Aunty Sara (Soper) and Uncle Jack Price (son of Jimmy's brother Bob Price), Violet, and Olive and children, Mac Lister and daughter.

22nd June... Short visit from Olive with glue and oilcloth for crutches. Mrs Holland called in for a moment. In evening Jack Graham came about fixing the car.
Wrote to Bob Henderson, Dave Welsh and Sister Bell.

23rd June... Saturday. Vera (& her 3 children, Athol, Valerie & Heather) called at 10.45am and took us to dinner at Lincoln. (name of Nelson's parents farm at Waianawa, then run by Dave's sons)
Went to Dave and Ollies for afternoon. Home 6pm. Quiet evening.

24th June... Went for afternoon tea at Thompson's Bush while kiddies at Sunday School. Picked them up afterwards and went to look at Caravan near railway. Jolly nice. Molly Henderson came.

25th June... Monday. Hospital in morning. Molly Henderson visits.
26th June... Dental examination in afternoon. Fixed handle on wood-box. Mrs Eric Smith in morning and Billy Milly in evening.

27th June... Hospital morning. Grace Graham short visit afternoon. Wilson Blakie and Molly Henderson in evening.

28th June... Morgan Clode, Mrs Bert Welsh and Evelyn came pm.

Here the diary of pre War, War, and post War activity ends.

--oo0oo--

PEGLEG: Soon after his return home Nelson became frustrated with the time it was taking to produce his artificial leg and he was sick of having to use crutches, so he made himself a 'pegleg leg' in his garage. He was soon walking unaided. Christopher remembers being told he held it in place holding a piece of string in his pocket.

Nelson's **ARMY MEDICAL RECORDS** show much activity through to 19 May 1945. The medical notes were in a sort of code, in brief words and some scribbled and hard to decipher ... starting ...

10 June 1944... Area 12 (Invercargill) to arrange treatment OPD Invercargill Kew Hospital. (Out Patients Dept)

(These hospital visits of 14, 16, 19, 21, 25, and 26 June 1944, we suggest were to have his right leg stump treated and bandaged until it healed, before making the artificial leg. T)

Lillian remembered the next seven months of surgery at Burwood, for treatment to his jaw and facial injuries.

8 July... Nelson travelled to Christchurch to Burwood Hospital, to be admitted to the Plastic Surgery Unit for treatment.

(I recall Mum telling me at some point that the Army paid all his train travelling and she could go free too. T)

31 August... Continue treatment PSU, Burwood. Remains on pay. Leave due 28 days.

4 October... Travel to PSU Burwood. Admitted 5 Oct.

Return home to convalesce for 2 months.

11 December… Return to Burwood PSU for treatment.
30 December… Sick at home. Area 11 to arrange with Area 12 for fitting of artificial limb at Dunedin Hospital. Remains on pay.
7 February 1945… Admitted to Montecillo Convalescence Home, Dunedin. Back home 8th.
17 April… to MCH, for fitting of artificial limb. Went home 21st.
1 May… to MCH, re new right leg. Went home 5 May.
16 May… Admitted to MCH and left there on the 19 May.
(Must have had his new leg on this trip as the report states…)
Area 12 Pool for discharge. Sick at home. 28 days Leave Due.
Pay ceases 23 June 1945.

………. End of Medical report ………..

7 August 1945… NELSON'S DISCHARGE CERTIFICATE.

Nº 17495

[Form N.Z.—748A.

NEW ZEALAND MILITARY FORCES

Certificate of Discharge

No. 471269 D. Rank: Private

Name (in full): Price Nelson

Pursuant to Regulation 40 (1a) of the National Service Emergency Regulations 1940, the above-named, having served outside New Zealand during the present war and having been found to be **medically unfit for active service** whether in New Zealand or elsewhere, and is unlikely to become fit for active service, is **discharged from the Armed Forces.**

The above-named, by reason of being discharged as aforesaid, is deemed to be transferred to the Third Division of the General Reserve constituted by the National Service Emergency Regulations 1940, and is therefore not liable, and should not apply, for enrolment in any class of such Reserve.

ARMY SERVICE.

In New Zealand (One) 1 years 277 days.
Overseas ——— years 326 days.

DESCRIPTION OF THE ABOVE-NAMED ON ENLISTMENT

Age: 31 years 194 days. Height: 6' 2"
Complexion: Fair Eyes: Grey
Hair: Dark Trade or occupation: Service Car Driver

Signature: [signature] Major
Adjutant-General,
New Zealand Military Forces.

Wellington, 7th August, 1945

—(1) This certificate is to be issued without any alteration in the manuscript.
(2) **WARNING.** The person to whom this certificate is issued should on no account part with it or forward it by post when applying for a situation, but should use a copy attested by a responsible person for the purpose. If this certificate is lost it will be replaced only when its loss can be proved to have been due to very exceptional circumstances. Applications for the replacement of a lost certificate should be made to Base Records, Wellington.
(3) ANY PERSON FINDING THIS CERTIFICATE is requested to forward it in an unstamped envelope to—
Base Records, Army Department, Wellington C.1, N.Z.

(Guess Nelson was now transferred onto the Government's Rehabilitation programme and the War Pension Scheme. T)

6 NOV 1944... AN AIR-GRAPH. It is a single page for brief messages. Kodak photo'd these and sent many on a roll of film to the Country (NZ) where they were printed and sent to the addressee. This minimized time and freight costs.

In this case "Christmas Wishes". The one below has the address clipped but it was sent to Nelson, from his 'Sergeant' in Italy with a reference to Nelson's Rural Delivery occupation before the Army and signed from his number 11 Platoon. Sent 6 Nov 1944 by his Sergeant Dave Welsh (now Warrant Officer second class. WO2)

Nelson received another Xmas air-graph from a war-mate, Private A M Miller, signed Mac ... see page 108.

NELSON'S 'WOODEN LEG'.

The first Army-supplied leg was held up by a large corset around his waist. Then along came a leg with fibreglass mould which his stump slid into and was held to his upper leg with velcro.

He enjoyed playing games with visiting children and grandchildren. Many still recall the tricks. He would undo the velcro then get them to help him pull his shoe off. He would tell them to pull harder and soon his whole leg would pop out of his trousers. We saw many startled kid's faces.

These 'wooden' legs all had breathing holes in the lower section and much to Lillian's displeasure he would take a pencil and ask a kid if they could do this … and he would thrust the pencil through his leg and out the other side. More gasps of surprise.

Lillian did not enjoy darning his socks. (C & T)

NELSON'S MEDALS and HAT BADGE:

This is the front view. From left to right they are ....

The 1939-1945 STAR: Navy Blue, Red, Light Blue ribbons.
The ITALY STAR 1943-45: Red, White, Green, White, Red.
1939-45 WAR MEDAL: Red, Blue, Red on white band, Blue, Red.
NZ WAR SERVICE MEDAL 1939-45: White, Black, White.

We have had these mounted for wearing at Anzac Parades, etc.

The reverse of the Stars are blank.
The 2 War medals show King George VI on the front and the NZ silver fern, and a Lion standing victorious over the enemy.

Nelson received these medals on 3 May 1950.

1994... CASSINO.

The International Anniversary Commemoration of the Monte Cassino battle, was held at Cassino, Italy and, aged 74 Nelson's Sergeant (Dave) David Caldwell Welsh DCM (#19863) attended.

He was awarded the DCM on 3 August 1944 and promoted at some point to Warrant Officer (WO2).

(Southland Times Newspaper)

DCM, stands for the Distinguished Conduct Medal, the oldest British Award for Bravery for Non Commisioned Officers.

--o0o—

The ARMY STRUCTURE:

A Corps has a Lt General (3 Star) and 20,000 to 45,000 men in 2 to 5 Divisions.

A Division has a Major General (2 Star) and 10,000 to 15,000 men. (in 3 to 4 Brigades)

A Brigade has a Colonel & 3,000 to 5,000 men. (2 to 3 battalions)

A Battalion has a Lt Colonel & up to 1,000 men. (4-6 Companies)

A Company has a Captain and up to 200 men. (3-4 platoons)

A Platoon has a Lieutenant (Lt) a NCO (Sgt) & up to 35 privates.

A Squad has 11 men .. a Sergeant and 10 men.

A Team has 4 men .. a Non Commisioned Officer and 3 men.

--o0o—

World War Two claimed the lives of 11,900 New Zealanders.

(National WW2 Museum)

--o0o—

Nelson's copy of the book ....

"26 BATTALION"

The New Zealand Official History of the 2nd NZEF

contains many of the comments and photos we have used to accompany Nelson's Diary record.

There are 12 pages in the back of the book listing all 459 men of the 2nd NZEF 26 Battalion, who died in World War II. Nelson has marked those he had grown to know, with red crosses beside their name ... probably for special thought on ANZAC days.

Pte. L. A. R. Wylie, of Seaward Downs, Southland, killed in action.

Pte. A. Richardson, of Mataura Island, Southland, killed in action.

Pte. W. E. S. Stevenson, husband of Mrs. A. L. Stevenson, Dunedin, died of wounds.

Pte. M. F. Donnelly, of Southland, killed in action.

Pte. F. H. Alderton, of Dunedin, killed in action.

Pte. F. W. Egan, of Mossburn, killed in action.

L/Sgt. I. Jenkins, of Winton, Southland, killed in action.

Sgt. G. L. Maze, of Balclutha, killed in action.

Pte. A. C. Emanuel, of Renwicktown, Marlborough, died of wounds.

2/Lt. A. A. McClean, of Invercargill, killed in action.

SERGEANT DAVID C. WELSH, of Ohai, who has been awarded the Distinguished Conduct Medal for courageous action and leadership at Cassino.

Ohai Soldier

AWARDED D.C.M.

Sergeant David Caldwell Welsh, of Ohai, has been awarded the Distinguished Conduct Medal for courageous action and leadership during the battle for Cassino, according to advice received by his wife, Mrs M. Welsh. Sergeant Welsh was wounded during the battle, but he has now recovered.

Sergeant Welsh is the second son of Mr and Mrs W. Welsh, of Ohai. He was born at Birchwood and educated at the Feldwick and Ohai schools. Sergeant Welsh was employed as a trucker by the Star Company before he joined the forces in 1941. He was a keen footballer and on one occasion represented the Southland schools at Dunedin. His elder brother is also serving overseas.

Mjr. R. S. Smith, of New Plymouth, killed in action.

Mjr. D. P. W. Harvey, of Rapaura, Blenheim, awarded the M.C.

Pte. S. J. Campbell, of Waipahi, killed

Cpl. W. G. Goodall, of Oamaru, died of wounds.

A page in Nelson's War photo album, records photos of some of his Army mates and Army leaders who did not return from the war, and some who gained reward for bravery.

Sergeant David Welsh was Nelson's sergeant in 11 Platoon.

Another person Nelson had time for was # 11 Platoon's Commander, Lieuetenant Alf McLean. (see page 59)

Many of these men were mentioned in Nelson's Diary.

EXPLANATIONS & ABBREVIATIONS:

(Military Termanology and Soldier Slang)

A.D.S.	Advanced Dressing Station. (First Aid)
AWOL	Absent without leave (permission)
Bde	Brigade (3 Battalions = 1 Brigade.)
B ECH	B Echelon ... generally area left out of battle, used to rest soldiers. Also refered as Rear Area.
BIVVY	Bivouac. 1 or 2 man 'tent' for temporary shelter.
BOFOR	Allied light anti-aircraft 40mm gun.
BREN	Allied light machine gun. Usually 1 Bren to 8-10 men. Was effective up to 600 yards.
BULLY	Tinned meat either beef or corned beef.
Capt	short for Captain.
C.O.	Commanding Officer.
Co or Coy	short for Company.
Cpl	short for Corporal.
Div. Cav.	Divisional Armoured Cavalry.
F.D.L.	Forward Defence Line.
FRUGAL	? Couldn't find. Suspect, code for when men were out on moving patrol on recci of enemy position.
GAT	US slang for pistol or revolver.
H.Q.	Head Quarters.
ITY	Slang for an Italian person.
GERRY, HUN or FRITZ	Slang for a German Soldier.
Lt or Lft	Short for Leuitenant.
LUGER	German soldier's pistol.
MORTAR	A muzzle loading weapon with a short barrel, that fires low-velocity shells over a short range.
N.C.O.	Non Commissioned Officer. (Sergeant etc)
NZGH	New Zealand General Hospital.
PANZER	At 55 tons this German Tank was almost twice as heavy as a NZ Sherman Tank.
PIAT	Projectile Infantry anti-tank gun. A 1 man weapon.

PIPPER 1, 2, 3, pips an shoulder epaulette = first or second Lieutenant and 3 = Captain.

POM Slang for anyone from the UK. (or Pommy)

PONGO Slang for British soldier. (Not used for Officer)

POW Prisoner of War.

PROVOST Army / Military Police.

R.A.P. Regimental Aid Post ... for triage and basic treatment of casualties.

ROADSTEAD Part of River/Sea where waiting ships wait.

RPM Rounds per minute.

RECCI Reconnaissance... observation of region.

SLITTY Slit Trench dug by soldier to give them protection.

SPANDAUS German machinegun. Could fire 1200 rounds per minute.

SHERMAN Allied medium size tank.

TELLER-MINE German circular steel cased mine buried in ground for tanks.

TOMMY Slang for English soldier or Officer.

WOG slang for Egyptian or other light skinned soldiers but not for Maoris. Alternatively thought to be .. Wily Oriental Gentleman.

YANKS Slang for American soldiers.

--o0o—

NELSON'S DIARY INDEX ... pages 4 to 115

NELSON'S DIARY INDEX page 2

NELSON'S DIARY INDEX page 3

ACKNOWLEDGEMENTS:

(AT) Alexander Turnbull Library, NZ.
(B) BALAGAN.info 2nd Division TIMELINE (Sangro River)
(F) Freyberg's War by Matthew Wright.
(G) General Lord Freyberg VC by Peter Singleton-Gates
(I) ITALY. Vol One by N C Phillips (Sangro to Cassino)
(N) NZ HISTORY (nzhistory.govt.nz)
(O) OFFICIAL HISTORY of 26 Battalion, NZ.
(W) WARRIOR NATION by John Thomson.
Auckland Library: Research Staff and records.
New Zealand National WW2 Museum.
Newpapers: Southland Times & Southland Daily News.
Finding book (G) ... Richard J Somerville
Proofreading and encouragement ... Jill V Price
(C) Nelson's Photo Albums, etc ... Chris T J Price
Publishing and computer help ... Tony J Price
Book Cover Design ... Xanthe R Price

Mum (Lillian) named this photo ... **"AT THE NURSERY"**
In 1935 Lillian's parents, Percy and Elsie Thomas, were living in the Thomas Bros Nursery house at Great North Road, Waikiwi, which was sited about where Bruce Street is in 2021.

Nelson 'courted' Lillian while she lived at the Nursery and they attended dances over the road a bit, at St Pauls Church Hall and in nearby village halls. He would travel to the dances on his motorbike from his parent's Waianawa farm.

They met at a Makarewa Hall dance in 1931, aged 21 & 19, were engaged in 1933 and married in 1935. (L)

NELSON, 3rd from left, was very proud to be selected for the

.... **WAIANAWA RUGBY TEAM**

The jersey colours were yellow and black, but seems a mixture here. (Nelson also played tennis in his youth.)

Waianawa district BOWLING GREEN and its formation.

POEM by Nelson's brother Dave Price.
Mentioned 9 lines down is the "Laird of Lincoln".

- The Bowling Green -

There's a stir at Lincoln Corner by the Monkey Puzzle tree,
Where the buffers of the district think a bowling green should be.
They believe a little action and a fiver here and there,
Would set the business going and they'd be without a care.
There is Andrew in his roughcast, only waiting it would seem,
To be honoured as the doner of this lovely bowling green.
'Dan the mover of this motion, with a fiver in his hand
Could be trusted with the upkeep and the limeing of this land.
--> And the robust Laird of Lincoln in a coat of tangerine,
When the roller needed mending, could be used to roll the green.

Nelson's father Jimmy Price owned and named "Lincoln Farm" at Waianawa, named after Lincolnshire in England, where his wife Hannah's mother Hannah Taylor Boyer was born. Jimmy was known at times as The Laird of Lincoln. He was fairly portly by this age and not as tall as Nelson, so the suggestion to use him as a roller was greatly enjoyed by Nelson and siblings.

All potential investors and members of the bowling green have received a mention.

Then there's Tom a bally good man, with a spade and shovel too,
He would surely drain the section and donate a guinea too.
Charles McCrostie from the forest would donate some shrubs, not dear;
And assist with all the planting and their trimming once a year.
Then there's Perry down at 'Mindork' has two guineas to be had,
Thinks the idea simply splendid and magnificent "by Gad".
Jimmie Brown could cart the timber to erect a bowlers seat,
And perhaps present a fiver; carting lambs is such a treat.
Father Forest down at 'Glenoak' has a pair of bowlers shoes,
He'd be very pleased to use them, after he has paid his dues.
Follow round to David Cartwright, he'd be there to do his share,
With his scissors in his pocket, to trim the bowlers hair.
Then of course there's Andrew Cartwright he'll be good for two fifteen,
With the right to graze his horses in the mornings on the green.
Next in line comes 'Davie Ewart who will be a bowler keen
In the latest square-cut blazer trimmed with blue and bottle green.
Then we come to Hunter brothers, they'll present a fiver each.
John to try to kiss the kitty, Hughie just to merely teach.
Last not least comes James McPherson, hes the daddy of them all,
Fairly gasping for the pleasure to present the banquet hall.
Now we have these trifles settled, time to bring the ladies in,
They'll be there, with tea and biscuits to try and make their husbands win,
There they'll hold their Mothers meetings; what the price of eggs will be.
How the calves and lambs are coming or going as the case may be.
And the hard worked sons and daughters of these buffers on the lawn
Will have many extra duties, just to keep their sires in form.
So perhaps we'd better leave them now that they've been shown the way
How to set a green in motion, they just pay and play away.

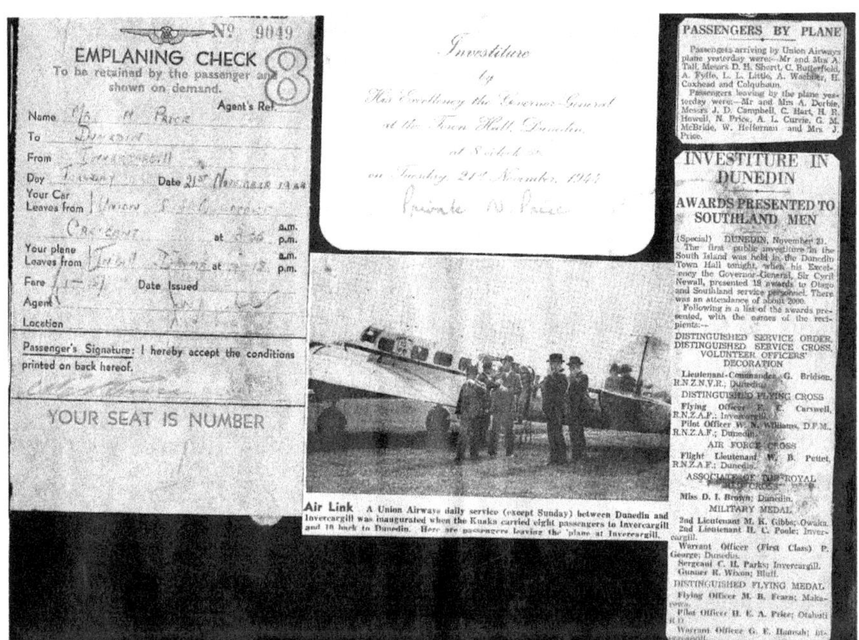

Nº 9049

EMPLANING CHECK

To be retained by the passenger and shown on demand.

Agent's Ref.

Name

To

From

Day

Date

Your Car Leaves from

at a.m. p.m.

Your plane Leaves from

at a.m. p.m.

Fare

Date Issued

Agent

Location

Passenger's Signature: I hereby accept the conditions printed on back hereof.

YOUR SEAT IS NUMBER

Investiture by His Excellency the Governor-General at the Town Hall, Dunedin, at 8 o'clock on Tuesday, 21st November, 1944

Private N. Price

Air Link A Union Airways daily service (except Sunday) between Dunedin and Invercargill was inaugurated when the Kuaka carried eight passengers to Invercargill and 10 back to Dunedin. Here are passengers leaving the 'plane at Invercargill.

PASSENGERS BY PLANE

Passengers arriving by Union Airways plane yesterday were:—Mr and Mrs A. Tall, Messrs D. H. Short, C. Butterfield, A. Fyffe, L. L. Little, A. Wachner, H. Coxhead and Colquhoun.

Passengers leaving by the plane yesterday were:—Mr and Mrs A. Derbie, Messrs J. D. Campbell, C. Hart, H. R. Howell, N. Price, A. L. Currie, G. M. McBride, W. Heffernan and Mrs J. Price.

INVESTITURE IN DUNEDIN

AWARDS PRESENTED TO SOUTHLAND MEN

(Special) DUNEDIN, November 21.

The first public investiture in the South Island was held in the Dunedin Town Hall tonight, when his Excellency the Governor-General, Sir Cyril Newall, presented 19 awards to Otago and Southland service personnel. There was an attendance of about 2000.

Following is a list of the awards presented, with the names of the recipients:—

DISTINGUISHED SERVICE ORDER, DISTINGUISHED SERVICE CROSS, VOLUNTEER OFFICERS' DECORATION

Lieutenant-Commander G. Bridson, R.N.Z.N.V.R., Dunedin.

DISTINGUISHED FLYING CROSS

Flying Officer F. E. Carswell, R.N.Z.A.F.; Invercargill.

Pilot Officer W. N. Williams, D.F.M., R.N.Z.A.F.; Dunedin.

AIR FORCE CROSS

Flight Lieutenant W. B. Pettet, R.N.Z.A.F.; Dunedin.

ASSOCIATE OF THE ROYAL RED CROSS

Miss D. I. Brown; Dunedin.

MILITARY MEDAL

2nd Lieutenant M. K. Gibbs; Owaka.

2nd Lieutenant H. C. Poole; Invercargill.

Warrant Officer (First Class) P. George; Dunedin.

Sergeant C. H. Parks; Invercargill.

Gunner R. Wixon; Bluff.

DISTINGUISHED FLYING MEDAL

Flying Officer M. B. Fearn; Makarewa.

Pilot Officer H. E. A. Price; Otahuti R.D.

Warrant Officer G. E. Hannah; Invercargill.

21 November 1944 ..... HAROLD'S INVESTITURE.

This is a page from Nelson's War Album. The photo shows Nelson attended an Investiture in Dunedin for the Southern Returned WW2 servicemen. His Invitation, His Emplaning Checkin Ticket and 2 newspaper records.

The small item mentions Nelson and his mother Mrs J (Hannah) Price.

The long item details Nelson's brother Harold's award **..... The DFM .....** **Distinguished Flying Medal, presented to Pilot Officer H E A PRICE** by the Governor-General Sir Cyril Newall. 19 Awards were presented with 2000 attendees.

--oo00oo--

NELSON's occupations. He worked on his father's farm at Waianawa until aged 23, had the Mail Run, drove Buses, graded Sheep. Each for about 15 yrs until retirment in 1975.

The MAIL RUN: 1932 to 1948.

The Times Newspaper article on page 20 shows a very diversified business with a huge staff, many in 1943 at WW2. Nelson's Rural Delivery run was the 'GORGE ROAD' area east of Invercargill, which he took up again after the War for a short time. Aged about 10-11 I went on one trip. A long day, up early, collect newspapers and mail and off we went with many gravel roads and dust. I recall being allowed to heave the pre-rolled plastic covered newspapers out the passenger's window, over the car cab and onto a driveway. I missed the drive the first time but was allowed 2 more throws with better result. Sometimes people would leave money and a shopping list for Dad. Mum would pop down to the Windsor shops, get the articles (cabbage, envelopes etc) and Dad would deliver them the next day complete with any change. Lillian helped with the accounts.

--oo0oo—

CHILDREN: Nelson and Lillian had 3 children.

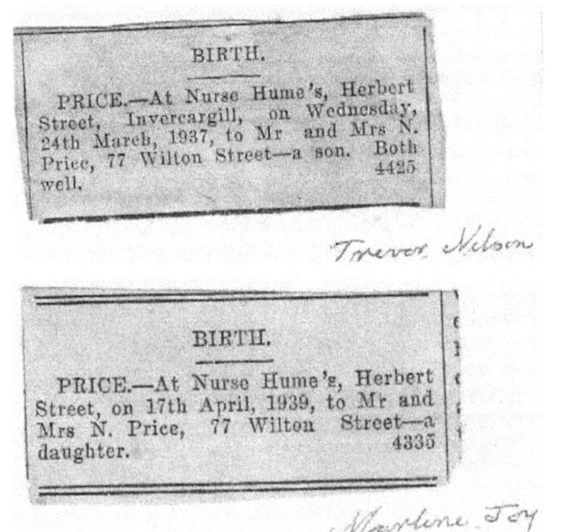

BIRTH.

PRICE.—At Nurse Hume's, Herbert Street, Invercargill, on Wednesday, 24th March, 1937, to Mr and Mrs N. Price, 77 Wilton Street—a son. Both well. 4425

Trevor Nelson

BIRTH.

PRICE.—At Nurse Hume's, Herbert Street, on 17th April, 1939, to Mr and Mrs N. Price, 77 Wilton Street—a daughter. 4335

Marlene Joy

During the years Nelson was on the Mail Run, Trevor 1937 and Marlene 1939 were born. The newspaper entry dosen't name us but Mum has added our names to her records.

When Christopher arrived in 1951 he received a silver cup being the first baby weighed in the new Waverly Plunket Rooms, Invercargill.

BUS DRIVER: 1948 to 1960.

This photo shows Nelson (on right) and one of the buses he was driving for the Tuffery Passenger Bus Services in Invercargill. (I do not know his companions)
I seem to recall his share of the city was the 'eastern route' out Tay Street to the city boundary at the Eastern Cemetery.
For a short time Nelson also drove the Invercargill Trams.

> Lillian recalled Mr Stan Gooseman ... then Government Minister of Transport, NZ, ... had advised them Nelson was the only Amputee holding a Passenger Bus Drivers Licence in New Zealand at that time.

Mr David W H Tuffery and wife Lilian owned the buses and operated out of premises at 189 Bamborough Road, Invercargill.

The ALLIANCE: 1960 to 1975.

Nelson became a full time employee of the newly built Alliance Freezing Works at Lornville in 1960. His job started out as Clerk to the slaughter board, recording weights and grades, of lambs and ewes on the chain. This information was recorded on a large pre-printed pad. Later when the volume increased and technology reached his work area the system changed. He was in charge of the Ticket Office. When lambs were weighed and graded a ticket was attached to each carcase recording these details and noted the particular exporter's name. This had to be done at the pace of 8 carcases per minute ... to match the speed of the slaughter chain. The Lornville works grew to 6 chains operating in the full season.

Nelson was in the ticket office and responsible for the ticket printing and supply for all six chains. He had them printed in Invercargill and sometimes he, Lillian and Chris would sit in an evening tying the strings to the tickets, ready for use.

As the works grew the jobs were separated and son Chris joined as a grader (a seasonal job) and all 6 chains had their own clerk and grader. The grade was determined by the fat content on the carcase's rib cage.

To get to his position on the top floor of the building Nelson had to climb 62 steps up and 62 down. His artificial leg sometimes broke at the ankle on these steps and he had to keep a spare leg in his locker for emergencies. Chris does not think any other employee had a spare leg in their locker at Lornville. (C)

This book **(A CUT ABOVE)** commemorates the early history of the **Alliance Freezing Works** in Southland.

There is a photo of all the staff gathering in 1975 to farewell retiring Chief Executive Ted Stanley on page 195, and Nelson can be found in the upper left-hand quarter of the photo.

After fifteen years service Nelson retired from the Alliance and was presented with this silver tray and jug. Lillian did not think it complete, so, went out and bought the tea-pot, milk jug and sugar bowl.

--oo00oo--

NELSON & LILLIAN'S FIRST HOME. 77 Wilton St.

(Google photo 2019) After their marriage in 1935 they moved into their new home at 77 Wilton St in North Invercargill.
Then, there was no house behind it, a garage at the end of a two concrete strip drive and two chimneys .. one in kitchen/living room for the coal range and open fireplace in the front lounge.
The front fence was 2 foot high (600mm) concrete rough-casted to match house and a beautiful cherry tree between drive and living room windows. The back yard consisted of lawn, clothesline, a hen house and run … which later was turned into a sand pit, and in the back left corner Dad had made an air-raid-shelter before he went off to war. He dug out six feet by two feet and two feet deep. Leaving a seat space each side, he used the soil for the sides with a sort of curved tin roof. A direct hit would have been disastrous. It used to fill with water … we were glad we never had to use it, however, we were pleased Nelson thought about some protection for us.
My sister Marlene and I were raised at 77 until our parents seemed to desire a larger home and at some point bought the section on the corner of Herbert and Exmouth Streets and sold

Wilton St. Thinking about it now, Mum probably hated the old coal range, the pantry with small meal preparation area, the single gas ring and the lack of kitchen cupboard space. (T)

420 HERBERT ST ... **Nelson & Lillian's home.**

This happened about 1948 and for two or three years we rented the house at 173 Bourke St. (Chris arrived when we were living there.) Together they designed and built this new mostly-electric home at 420 Herbert St, where they lived the rest of their lives. A large kitchen with breakfast table and lots of cupboards and a dining/living room next to it, three double bedrooms, a front lounge and a large garage for 2 cars and Nelson's various large and small tools. They were one of the first to use the 'McKay Space Heaters'. (2 of them) From the plans I estimate house 1480 square feet and garage 575. Nelson, in his spare time erected first the garage and then the house. I recall at least one day mixing concrete while Dad poured it into concrete block frames. Another day I helped remove set blocks and turn others over to dry. Quite heavy and solid. I enjoyed being allowed to measure, cut and nail Rimu dwangs beween the wall studs. Was very hard timber and I was slow. I was invited for only a few days.

Nelson was greatful to Bill Murray (a builder) who lived a few doors away and willingly answered Nelson's questions when he got stuck with how to do something. I recall Mum and Dad had many discussions and trials about how to curve the plywood to make the multi-curved front entrance wall unit.
The garage was reinforced poured concrete and I have no idea how Dad got up to the upper levels with a wheel barrow or bucket of concrete, on his 'wooden leg'. No ready-mixed pumped concrete then. This building housed the bus they converted into a mobile caravan, and later his speed boats, but started off filled with all the tools, timber, cement, windows etc, needed for the house construction.
Soon after 1960 Mum decided to update the front garden and sent me this plan (NTS) to see what was going to happen. She must have learnt something while living at her father's nursery. I was impressed but living in Auckland I could not help her. When he was aged 80 Nelson painted the roof. He tied himself up there and scooted about on his backside. He rigged up a rope

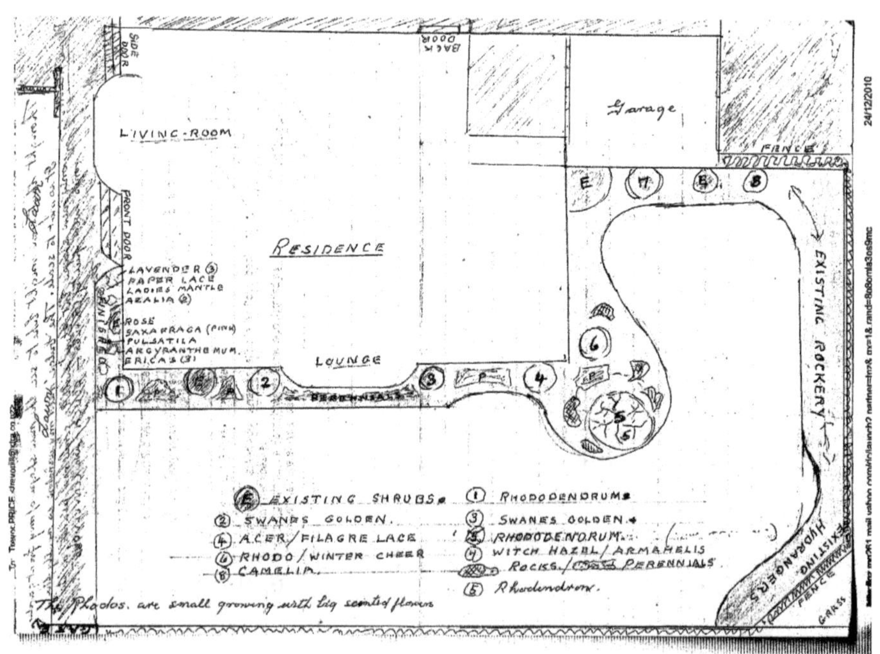

and bucket system for Lillian to send up his cuppas and lunch. (toilet? another story) He didn't come down until he finished.(T)

NELSON'S HOBBIES:

In the early days at 420 Nelson had a **WOOD-LATHE** in the garage and turned out many things such as candle-stick-holders, bread boards, all different size bowls. Some of these Mum donated to the Waverly Church for their fund raisers and family got some too. Then he started to laminate different coloured wood to produce very interesting bowls. All completed in varnish. Photo shows a little one that I have, measuring 85mm diameter by 42mm high. Has been used to hold milk tokens and paper clips.

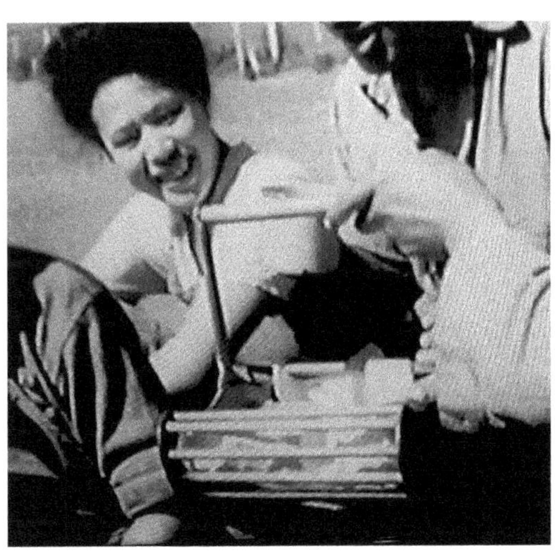

He also mass produced a wooden BASKET that was then fashionable and sold them cheaply to the ladies of the Waverly Presbyterian Church where Lillian was on a number of clubs and committees. Made of plywood sides and base, with dowl ends and handle. I think Mum decorated the sides with flowers, then varnished. This photo from google shows the baskets but with taller handles than those Nelson made.

CARS, CARAVANS, TRAILERS, MOTOR BIKES, BOATS etc

Nelson sold his bench saw, band saw, wood planner and turned his garage into a repair shop.

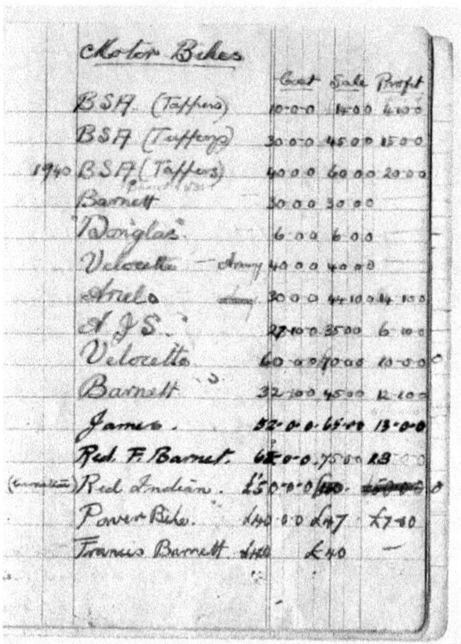

Motor Bikes

	Cost	Sale	Profit
BSA (Taffers)	10-0-0	14-0-0	4-0-0
BSA (Taffers)	30-0-0	45-0-0	15-0-0
1940 BSA (Taffers)	40-0-0	60-0-0	20-0-0
Barnett	30-0-0	30-0-0	
Douglas	6-0-0	6-0-0	
Velocette — Army	40-0-0	40-0-0	
Ariel	30-0-0	44-10-0	14-10-0
A J S.	27-10-0	35-0-0	6-10-0
Velocette	60-0-0	70-0-0	10-0-0
Barnett	32-10-0	45-0-0	12-10-0
James	52-0-0	65-0-0	13-0-0
Red F. Barnet	62-0-0	75-0-0	13
Red Indian	£50-0-0	[illegible]	[illegible]
Power Bike	£40-0-0	£47	£7-0-0
Francis Barnett	£40	£40	—

These took up a lot of his after work, evenings and weekend time. He bought cars, motorbikes, caravans and trailers, fixed whatever he found wrong with them, cleaned them inside and out, sometimes repainted them, and when sold hopefully made a profit. Most car engines were water-blasted and painted chrome colour and if necessary exteriors were painted in his favourite combination of dark emerald green, with black mudguards. Photos show records from the back of his war-diary. I recall the motor registration people saying that if he changed ownership more than 6 times a year he would be classed as a 'trader' and would have to pay tax etc. He reduced the volume of activity.

Cars

	Cost £ s d	Sale £ s d	Profit
Baby Austin Tourer	45-0-0	55-0-0	10-0-0
Chev. Tourer	60-0-0	70-0-0	10-0-0
Dodge 1930 Sedan	120-0-0	150-0-0	30-0-0
Morris 12 HP 1936	235-0-0	275-0-0	40-0-0
Chev. 6 - 1934	300-0-0	345-0-0	45-0-0
De Soto DeLux 1936	305-0-0	310-0-0	5-0-0
Hillman Minx 10HP 1937	305-0-0	320-0-0	15-0-0
Chev. DeLux 1937	365-0-0	440-0-0	45-0-0
Hudson Super 6. 1929	100-0-0	165-0-0	65-0-0
Graham Paige 1930	180-0-0	195-0-0	15-0-0
New Beauty Ford 1920	35-0-0	45-0-0	10-0-0
Model A.A. Ford 1931	180-0-0	205-0-0	25-0-0
Oldsmobile 1935	400-0-0	500-0-0	100-0-0
Morris 12 1936	445-0-0	465-0-0	20-0-0
Morris 12 [illegible]	460-0-0	490-0-0	30-0-0
Chev. 1936	525-0-0	555-0-0	30-0-0
Oldsmobile	410-0-0	430-0-0	20-0-0
Humber 1939	460-0-0	495-0-0	35-0-0

Trailers and Caravans

	Cost £ s d	Sale £ s d	Profit £
Folding Caravan	35-0-0	55-0-0	20
4 Bunk Caravan	65-0-0	120-0-0	55
DeLux Caravan	200-0-0	310-0-0	110
Trailer	25-0-0	45-0-0	20
Caravan [illegible]	280-0-0	375	95
Caravan [illegible]	£350	£310	X
Mobile Super Caravan & Awning [illegible]	£235		

TWO AUSTIN SEVENS. Trevor's at left I think was a 1927-29 and Nelson's was the soft top in front ... both in the green/black colouring. My love of speed cost me plenty and in the end Dad fitted a cotton reel between my foot and the floor boards. I had three Austin Sevens over the years and dad bought others for parts to keep them going. I paid for parts but labour was free.

Nelson became interested in **GO-KARTS.** He and Chris tried these out at Oreti Beach and the Southland Go-Kart Track but never raced. Karts had to be push started usually by running behind, but Nelson towed them behind his car. Much easier. (C)

SPEED BOATS. Lillian records Nelson was always interested in sport and deer stalking, duck shooting, clay-bird shooting, whitebaiting and gold prospecting.
Chris, when aged 13-15, advises Nelson owned 2 different racing speed boats over the years which together they drove to some success. 'FAIRLINE' was a flat bottom boat and 'SILVER SPRAY' a hydroplane model. Nelson joined the Southland Power Boat Club and won a few trophies that had to be handed back for next years racing. Mostly they raced on the Oreti River

but once in Riverton harbour, once at Lakes Te Anau and Waihola. At 420 Nelson restored and painted the Boat Club's tractor that was used to put boats into and out of the water. (C)

Nelson showing off ***Fairline*** to grandchildren Jeffrey and Tony, and Trevor had a short drive.

Silver Spray, very sleek, and, after hitting the wake of a boat on Oreti River. It needed a big repair job. Lots of fibreglass required but then it was a very useful filler of all the problems he found in various cars and boats. Nelson enjoyed the repairs and improvements he made to these vehicles. (C)

I recall him buying a car axel once and travelling all over Invercargill to buy parts and to completely make up a trailer. (T)

NELSON HAD 2 PETS.

His dog Gary was a hunting dog ... and only he was allowed near it. A Golden Retriever who went on most of his trips especially to get ducks, and deer. But his budgie sat in its cage beside him in the Living room at 420. It was allowed out to fly about the room and made a lot of noise. Generally about tea time Nelson covered the cage to make the bird think it was dark and time to keep quiet. It did not get the message and often chirped away during a programme he was watching on TV. Dad would pick up the newspaper and hit the cage ... and the bird would be quiet.
Here he is introducing his budgie to granddaughter Hannah.

This photo shows the Camper with Chris and Gary. The other shows Trevor feeding the hens at 77 Wilton St.

CLAY BIRD SHOOTING:

In an Army Platoon there are two men who need to be Bren Gun operators. They worked as a pair, one to shoot and the other as a sighter and to carry extra Bren ammo etc, and take over the Bren should anything happen to No.1.

Nelson was number 2 in the Bren Gun team. His Diary often mentioned, him oiling and cleaning, and protecting their Bren and their rifles.

How were they selected ?

We guess it was results on the firing range in NZ, where the men were taught to shoot with their 303 rifles and the Bren. It could be Dave Parr was a better shot, or, they were equal and because Dave being so slight (page 23) and Nelson a big bloke, this settled their positions. Nelson didn't record that.

Nelson's Diary records 11 shooting prizes he won .... including the silver cup shown here engraved ... **LINCOLN HANDICAP CLAY BIRD MATCH, won by NELSON PRICE.**

(Sounds as if Nelson's father sponsored this shoot at his farm.)

No date on the CUP or in his Diary! As it's in the Diary, maybe it was after 13 June 1944. Here is the list of winnings ....

Half dozen Tea Spoons (3rd in The Bluff Championship)

Half dozen Knives (2nd at Bluff)

Silver Cup (1st Lincoln Open Shoot)
Double yellow Pyrex Dish (1st Grassmere Open Shoot)
Christmas Cake (11th Grassmere Xmas Shoot)
2 Pounds (2nd Grove Bush Open Shoot)
25 Shillings (tied first Gorge Road Open Shoot)
1 Pound (Best Shot at Tuatapere)
Clock (1st Grove Bush Open Shoot)
18 Pounds (1st Grassmere Xmas Shoot) and same day …
6 Pounds (1st Grassmere Sweepstake)

Nelson's father Jimmy **(James McDonald Price)** was a good shot … he belonged to the Athol Gun Club … and on 2 November 1907 he won this medal.

This Price families **3rd generation** aged 16, had a brief experience in shooting but did not continue with it.

MRS T. BLEE took top honours at the weekly shoot of the Home Services Club with 100.8. Next were **J. CONNELL** and **S. RIZZI** with 99.8, followed by **A. POMEROY** 99.7, **T. CRANE** 99.6, **G. HOWIE** 99.5 and **MISS JORDAN** 99.5. In the B grade, **J. OGILVEY**, having his first shoot for two years, took the honours with 98.7.

Next in line were **L. PADGET** 96.3, **E. GRAFTON** 97.5. The **PATTERSON** brothers showed great promise for beginners, and scored 91.2 each, thus taking the honours in the C grade. **T. PRICE**, 88.1, was next, and although only a lad, he shows great promise.

Rifle Shooting

28-5-53

HOMESERVICEMEN MEMBERS RETURN FOUR POSSIBLES

Members of the Homeservicemen's Rifle Club were in top form this week, returning four possibles. The consistent J. Connell took the honours with 100.7 being one inner in front of Mrs T. Blee.

Results:

A Grade: J. Connell 100.7, Mrs T. Blee 100.6, E. Grieber 100.5, A. Pomeroy 100.5.

B Grade: A. Jordan 97.6, G. Howie 96.5.

C Grade: M. Millar 93.1, A. Walker Jnr. 92.2. J. Patterson 92.2, T. Price 90.2.

--oo00oo--

NELSON'S CAMPER

The July/August 2004 issue of NZMCA's 'The Motor Caravanner', pages 73-76 displayed the No 1 Bulletin of the 'NZ Motor Caravan Assn', as sent to the members in 1958.

With pride I found my father listed on page 74 ... "Mr N (Nelson) Price of Invercargill" and it seems he was member number 6, with Andy Anderson not listed, as number 1. The article states that Andy Anderson started the NZMCA in March 1956. Nelson was the first Southlander and second South Islander to join.

About 1947 Nelson purchased an old side-loader bus which had been retired from the NZR Road Services. With 4 doors down the side, passengers used to climb in and slide over the bench seats to the far window with more people following the first person in. With 4-5 people per seat, all had to exit if the first in wanted off the bus. Nelson ripped out all the bench seating and sent the bus off to have the roof raised. He was 6'2" tall and the bench seat system allowed very little height.

My mother, Lillian, designed the layout for the interior and after Nelson welded up two of the doors, they together made and fitted it all. Wardrobe, cupboards, seating etc. It took quite some time to do the conversion as Nelson only had his evenings and the weekends to work on it. At 12 years of age I was not really into mechanical and building work and they were probably thankful I was seen but not heard. Two items I recall and admired were the front seating and my bed. The front seat was a three way thing. The two parts were a full width bench of ply with wood frame and foam cushioning held together and to the floor, with large tower bolts, to provide driving comfort and safety for driver and two passengers. My sister Marlene usually sat up front with my mother and I sat in the back area. When in camp they could fold the back down to make a double bed and as it was on skids it could be converted into a daytime seat facing into the camper space. Ingenious, eh! My sister and I had a three foot wide seat under the rear side windows which converted into a 5 foot bed. We had to remove the foam squab and open a cupboard door at the rear end of the seat. This cupboard had a foam base and was about 2 feet deep and provided space to put our feet when it was sleep time. These cupboards also kept our pyjamas, blankets and pillows out of sight in the daytime.

The heating and means of cooking were on a small pot-bellied stove near the entrance door and we found it too hot to use in the daytime and was soon only lit about dusk. After our South Island trip the stove was removed and a cap fitted over the roof hole, I can't recall what replaced the stove. We always stayed in campgrounds where showers, toilets and kitchens were available. Dad also fitted a canvas awning to the camper's side where needed but not always used stuff, was stored when in a camp.

During the school-holidays 1949/50 we started our South Island tour up the east coast and I remember in Ashburton we were made to feel like royalty, with people oohing and ahhing over the camper. We had stopped in the main shopping street and found something for lunch when a gent approached and wanted to see over the camper. Said he was a journalist. Mum and Dad were happy to do this and he took lots of notes and photos, then made us line up alongside the camper and took another photo. He reckoned he would get an article published and call it "Camping of the Future". Although spending many recent hours searching through the Ashburton, Christchurch newspapers and the Auckland Weekly News I have not found this article and it is not in mother's various family scrap books. I remember waving to those that stopped and stared at the camper as we left Ashburton. We did Christchurch, Picton, Nelson and spent some time admiring the pancake rocks and blow holes on the West Coast. When we arrived at Greymouth it was raining cats and dogs, and after Mum got us a park-up spot in the campground, Dad was in and out of the camper, 4 or 5 times in the rain, placing planks of wood under the tyres to get the camper level. Finally he was inside and drying himself off and Mum was preparing tea, when she said

"Oh, I've forgotten to get milk." Dad said "Bugger the milk." There was no way he was going to drive off to get some. We went on to look around Hokitika and saw the glaciers. Another year we visited the Hermitage and saw Mt Cook and a trip of two free-camping nights at Lake Monowai where Dad spent a day deer stalking. The camper was used most years on much shorter trips and lent sometimes to friends. I have no idea where it is now.

For the vehicle buffs the bus was a 1933-35 American Reo, which had had a British Bedford motor fitted some years before Dad bought it. I need to thank the many people of a number of NZ clubs and organisations who helped me identify the special wheel design, the radiator grille shape and the badge attached. There were 2 different number plates in other old photos but of no use to identify the vehicle and only the odd photo has lasted the years.

Terms like Mobile Home, Motorcaravan, and Campervan were not in use then and we just called it The Camper. Dad was member number 6 of the NZMCA, and my wife Jill and I are number 17044 and someday we hope one of our children will join up and enjoy all the benefits of the present version of the NZMCA which we have seen grow over the years and enjoyed ourselves in our caravan. We still enjoy travelling, in our fourth caravan. We also enjoy the Travel Directory and The Motor Caravanner which causes arguments when it arrives, as we both want to read it first. I seem to always get second look.

I am no longer 12 but much older and can't wait to get away to a few of the NZMCA camps this coming summer.

Trevor Price.

The editor of The NZMCA 'Motor Caravanner' took this letter and turned it into a story as if I had been interviewed and added pictures which I show on the next page. Very clever of him and nothing was added or missed out.

This story and these photos appeared in the NZMCA magazine "The Motor Caravanner" Issue 346 of Aug / Sept 2020.

The former Road Service's bus that Nelson Price (#6) and his wife Lillian converted into a camper for their family in the late-1940s.

CLOCKWISE FROM ABOVE: *Trevor Price's Dad Nelson proudly stands alongside his camper. The young lad is Trevor's younger brother Christopher in about 1954; Nelson's camper with awning and chimney and Lilian in the deckchair; Jill and Trevor Price (#17044) gold prospecting somewhere up a West Coast river; Jill and Trevor's present caravan (their fourth) at the NZMCA Park at Parnassus.*

--oo0Ooo--

GOLD PROSPECTING

Throughout his retirement he enjoyed gold prospecting and was often away trying new spots mentioned by friends and relations. His Soper cousins had had gold claims at Garston and The Nevis and he had to see if they left any.

He had an old Commer van in which he slept and carried cooking equipment and a good food supply. On one rainy day we found him at a public space with toilets and a sign "No Camping". He was lying in bed reading waiting on the rain to stop. Been there two days. When Lillian joined him on these adventures he towed her small 3 m caravan.

He also tried his luck at many places ... a few being Arrowtown, The Gibson Valley, at Waikaia, and on the West Coast too, based in Blackball trying all the rivers close by.
He was always looking for new ideas on how to gather gold and once took his trailer to collect a system from a chap in Nelson.
This was an interest he shared with son Trevor and Jill, their family and Jill's mother Edna. They all often met up over the Christmas /New Year holidays.

PHOTO: Nelson in usual gold prospecting attire complete with steel bar and shovel. An old 'wooden leg' was premanently fitted into the long wellies.

NELSON SHIFTING BOULDERS WITH LILLIAN

BELOW ... Nelson joined his two riffle-boxes together and with son Trevor shovelled river gravel over them collecting Waikaia gold. A great day together.
While I took this photo he is standing in my area.

He was left handed and I am right handed, so .. the setup was perfect. He had a pump to get the water up and over the boxes.

Here he is some years later back at the same river, with a new wider box, accompanied by Lillian who is panning out some wash and Chris is reading.

--oo0Ooo--

Nelson, two years before he died.

Christmas 1991 with son Christopher's family:

Back ...	Nelson 81, Christopher 40, Trevor 54.
Middle ...	Lillian 79 and Esther 33.
Front ...	Jonathan 8, Hannah 6, Matthew 9.

Nelson had this photo in his War Album? Daughter Marlene and Noel Gorrie with children Ritchie, Lianne and Raewyn.

TODD'S AUCTION ROOMS:

Invercargill's auction rooms held auctions once a week and Nelson usually attended. Once when I was visiting I went along. He was warmly greeted by the managment and staff and seemed to know almost everyone else there. Lots of chats with people. We viewed mechanical stuff, old farm equipment, a tractor, two sheep, some hens, and rows of general household bits and pieces. It seems Nelson bought large boxes of books now and then and he bought one that day. He and Lillian would read what they wanted to from the box, then he would take it back and resell that lot, selecting a new box to bid for.

TELEVISION:

Chris reminded me Nelson was into TV right from the start. He erected a very tall aerial pole near the front door and purchased a TV. All was black and white to start with (1969) and sometimes not the best reception. Friends sometimes popped in to view. Chris recalls one night (1973-75) when they watched television while eating tea, it suddenly changed to colour. They were astonished, as they did not know Nelson had bought a colour television set. (C)

GARDENING:

Nelson was not really into flowers and shrubs but had a large vegetable and potato area. Each year he would dig in a trailer load or two of seaweed from Oreti beach and grew enough spuds that lasted the year. He also erected his own glass house where mostly tomatoes were grown. Lillian tended the flower sections but Nelson helped with any heavy work she needed and mowed the lawns. They both liked things tidy.

Nelson's Obituary ... he died 25 June 1993 (82)

Nelson Price

Overcame odds

With the death in Southland Hospital last week of Nelson Price at the age of 82, Invercargill lost a personality who will be long remembered for his achievements as a one-legged war veteran.

He never regarded his loss of a leg as a serious disability and it never deterred him from venturing into rough and remote country in pursuit of his favourite hobby, gold fossicking.

Mr Price was born at Athol, the son of James and Hannah Price, in a house built in 1899 by his pioneer grandfather, Morgan Price. He played rugby and tennis and was president of the sports club in 1932.

After moving to Invercargill, he bought the Gorge Road rural delivery, which he ran until 1948. This period was interrupted when he went overseas during World War II. He was wounded twice in Italy and lost his right leg below the knee.

On his return to New Zealand he found the delay in obtaining an artificial leg frustrating, so he made one himself.

Sheer determination saw him walking and driving again and back at work on his mail run. In 1948 the mail run was sold and Mr Price began driving buses until 1960.

After selling their Wilton Street home Mr Price and his wife, Lillian, bought an empty section in Herbert Street. There they built their dream house.

In 1957 he became secretary of the Tramways Union for a year and then went to work at the newly opened Alliance freezing works. He retired from there in 1975.

Mr Price is survived by his wife and sons Trevor, of Auckland, and Chris, of Invercargill. A daughter, Marlene, died in 1988.

(Sorry, do not know who wrote this. Could have been myself, Mum or F W G Miller who was a family friend)

Lillian died 2 January 1999 (86)

Nelson and Lillian were interred side by side at the "Garden of Rest" area, plot number 4, at the Southland Crematorium, off Rochdale Road, Invercargill.

Nelson and Lillian's daughter
MARLENE JOY GORRIE
nee Price 1939 – 1988.

NELSON and LILLIAN'S WEDDING:

18 Nov 1935 at Invercargill.

St Stephen's Presbyterian Church, Waikiwi, Invercargill.

Lillian's brother Hector in middle row, with her best life-long friend cousin Jessie Hockings, and her brother Leslie at rear, with Nelson's sister Nancy.

Jessie Hockings : Lillian : Nelson's sister Nancy ... at Nursery.
And later at the Nursery, and in their going away attire.

Chris and Esther's copy of the 'going- away' photo is hand painted by Lillian. She is wearing a Fur Fashion Wrap, and on the back is written ... *'Dress henna and brown, Nel in going-away rig. Blue forget-me-not boarder'.* (C)

Married 18 November 1935 at Invercargill.

GOLDEN WEDDING ANNIVERSARY :
18 November 1985 at home ... 420 Herbert St, Invercargill.
(photo completely framed by son Chris for Xmas 1985.)

Nelson's Parents .... Unknown photo date.
Married 5 April 1899 at Lumsden, Southland, NZ.

Lillian's parents ....
Married 9 November 1908 at Waterton, Ashburton, NZ.

NEW ZEALAND

COPY OF REGISTER OF MARRIAGE BY

1935. Marriage in the District of

No.	When and where married. (Date, Description of Building, and Locality.)	Names and Surnames of the Parties.	Ages.	Rank or Profession.	Condition of Parties:— 1. Bachelor or Spinster (or as case may be). If Widower or Widow, 2. Date of Decease of former Wife or Husband.
135	November 18th 1935 In St. Stephen's Presbyterian Church, Waikiwi	Nelson Price	24	Mail contractor	1. Bachelor 2.
		Lillian Elsie Thomas	23	Domestic	1. Spinster 2.

Married, after the delivery to me of the Certificate required by the Marriage Act, 1908, by

This marriage was solemnized between us, Nelson Price, Lillian Elsie Thomas

In the presence of us, Jessie Hockings, Hector Percival

I certify that the above is a true copy of the entry in the Register-book of Marriages kept by me

Registrar's Certificate No. 256 District of Invercargill

Nelson and Lillian's wedding certificate .. continues over →

1036 [R.G.—3B.

NEW ZEALAND.

CERTIFICATE OF DATE OF BIRTH.

I HEREBY CERTIFY that, according to the record of the birth in my office. Nelson Price was born at Athol on the 6th December day of 1910,

Deputy Registrar of Births and Deaths for the District of Lumsden

Dated at Lumsden this 24th day of February, 1931

(THE FEE FOR THIS CERTIFICATE IS ONE SHILLING.)

Nelson's Birth Certificate.

D. [R.G.—12.

Y OFFICIATING MINISTER.

Invercargill

Birthplace.	Residence. 1. Present. 2. Usual.	PARENTS. (1) Father's Name and Surname. (2) His Rank or Profession.	(1) Mother's Name. (2) Her Maiden Surname.
Athol	1. Invercargill 2. Invercargill	1. James Price 2. Farmer	1. Hannah Price 2. Loper
Ashburton	1. Waikiwi 2. Waikiwi	1. Percival Wallis Thomas 2. Nurseryman	1. Elsie Maud Thomas 2. Stevens

W. J. Robertson, Officiating Minister.

108 Grey St. Ashburton Dressmaker

Thomas. Nurseryman. Waikiwi

at St. Stephen's Manse, Waikiwi Invercargill

W. J. Robertson
Officiating Minister.

Denominaton: Presbyterian

balance of Wedding Certificate & Nelson's School Certificate

[B.—9.

NEW ZEALAND.—EDUCATION DEPARTMENT.

CERTIFICATE OF ATTAINMENT.

This is to certify *that* NELSON PRICE

of Waianiwa *School, in the Education District of* Southland, *has satisfied the requirements for a Certificate of Attainment in the* Fifth *Standard.*

(Signed) [signature]

Official designation: Secretary.

Date: 24th February, 1931. [OVER.

NEW ZE

CERTIFIED COPY of ENTRY in the REGISTER-BOOK of BIR

No.	Child.			Parents.	
	When and where born.	Name of Child, and whether present or not.	Sex.	Father. 1. Name and Surname. 2. Rank or Profession. 3. Age. 4. Birthplace.	When and where married.
5405	3rd August 1912 Grey Street Ashburton	Lilian Elsie not present	f.	1 Percival Walter Thomas 2 Produce Merchant 3 30 4 Christchurch	9th November 1908 Waterton

I hereby certify that the above is a true copy of an entry of birth in the Register-book kept in

Given under my hand ________ at ASHBURTON. this

[Fee payable: 2s. 6d., Ordinar

Lillian's birth certificate .... continues below
(Although it's Lilian on her certificate, she used Lillian.)

EALAND.

2427

THS in the District of ASHBURTON.

[R.G. No. 3E.

Mother. 1. Name and Maiden Surname. 2. Age. 3. Birthplace.	Informant. 1. Signature. 2. Description. 3. Residence. 4. If Entry a Correction of a Former Entry, Signatures of Witnesses attesting the same.	Registrar. 1. When registered. 2. Signature of Registrar.	Child. Name, if added or altered after Registration of Birth.
1 Elsie Maud Thomas formerly Stevens 2 27 3 Ashton	1 P. W. Thomas 2 Father 3 Ashburton	1 11th September 1912 2 W. W. White Registrar	

n my office.

9th day of February, 1927

W. W. White
Registrar.

ry Copy; 5s., Copy under Seal.]

NELSON and the NUMBER 6 ...

While gathering information for my various Price family books I became interested in the way **6th December** and the **number 6** often popped up as part of Nelson's history.

6 DECEMBER ....

1910 Nelson was born on this date in 1910 at Athol, NZ.

1857 Nelson's grandparents W D Soper married Hannah Taylor Boyer at Cathcart, NSW, Australia on this date.

1867 Nelson's gandparents, John Morgan Price married Jane McDonald at Riverton, Southland, NZ, on this date.

1868 Nelson's Aunty Hellen was born on this date at Athol. (1st born child of Morgan and Jane Price)

1872 Section 7 of Athol (10 acres) was registered to Nelson's grandfather Morgan Price on this date.

1942 Nelson's father Jimmy gave him his Browning automatic shotgun on this date for his 32nd birthday.

1942 Nelson's father James McDonald Price aged 66, died on this date, at "Lincoln Farm", Waianawa, Southland.

THE NUMBER 6.

1910 Nelson was the **6th child** of J McD & Hannah Price and his name ... Nelson ... has **6 letters**.

1944 6th February. Nelson trod on a mine in Italy and lost a leg.

1869 Nelson's grandfather JMP bought his first 10 acre block of land at Athol named **Section 6.**

Nelson's grandmother **Jane Price,** died at Athol aged 66 in 1909.

420 Herbert St, Invercargill. Those numbers add up to 6.

NZMCA. Nelson was the **sixth person** to join the organisation that is now known as New Zealand Motor Caravan Association.

NZMCA. My article about "Nelson's Camper" which appeared in the NZMCA Aug/Sept 2020 magazine ... was mentioned in the Index on **page 6** and the article itself starts on **page 66.**

Son Trevor & Jill lived at **6 Walter St**, Takapuna for about 50 yrs.

1993 Nelson had a stroke and spent some weeks in **Ward 6** at Kew Hospital, Invercargill where he died.

FAMILY PHOTO:

From left ... Jill holding Janene, Lillian, Chris, Nelson, Marlene holding Ritchie, and Noel, with Raewyn and Lianne in front.

Photo probably dated September 1970 at Invercargill.

If date correct, ... Janene aged 11 months, Jill 29 years, Ritchie 4 and shy, Marlene 31, Noel 32, Raewyn 10, Lianne 8, Chris 18, Lillian 58 and Nelson 59.

The only special family occasion that fits that date is Jill's brother Dick's marriage in Dunedin. Jill and Janene visited Invercargill after this event to introduce Janene to all her southern relations. Trevor was working in Auckland while Jeff and Tony were living over the road with the Taylor family.

Kyla joined Marlene and Noel's family a year later in Oct 1971.

The photographer was Jill's mother Edna Somerville.

LILLIAN'S FATHER .... PERCY THOMAS:

Percy enjoyed gardening and was well suited for the role of Nursery owner with his brother Jack at Invercargill. He had two hobbies I am aware of .... Photography and Painting.

Unfortunately, after he died, his wife Elsie felt that all their photos and other items were private and no one else would be interested or need to know of them and they were destroyed.

This is a photo I have of Percy aged about 21, (in 1902) and his signature is on this landscape oil painting, measuring 400 wide x 580mm tall.

This is Percy's metal paint box produced by Winsor & Newton of London. All the paints have hardened up and useless now.

LILLIAN .... Ashburton to Invercargill:

When Percy Thomas' brother Jack saw a business opportunity in Invercargill he asked Percy to leave Ashburton and join him in purchasing Lennie's Nursery at Waikiwi, (was near to Bruce St) Invercargill. Percy was to run the nursery and Jack soon opened a shop in the cities 'Briscoes' building in Dee St, Invercargill to sell their Nursery produce.

Lillian was now 12, and with her parents, brothers Hector and Leslie, left Ashburton 20 January 1925. They moved into the Thomas Brothers Nursery house on April 8. Lillian finished her education at Southland Technical College then worked at the Nursery. The Nursery land today is covered in housing.

> (At some point Lillian won a swimming medal and it may have been at this college as no record of her win appears in the Ashburton newspapers. I have never seen the medal but it is known about within the family.)

When the Nursery was sold Percy bought a small Dairy on the northern side of West Plains Road that backed on to the railway line. They moved in 4 December 1935. Lillian married Nelson in November 1935. The shop is no longer there.

In January 1940 they sold up and retired to a house at 34 Huia St, Waikiwi, where Percy had a large garden. I recall visiting often and being allowed to roam the garden, finding bamboo pieces 200-300mm long that earwigs loved to hide in during the daytime. I had a small bucket half full of hot water and emptied the earwigs from the bamboo into it. None survived and Granddad's leafy vegetables didn't get holes in them for a while.

Percy found time to play bowls and the Waikiwi Bowling grounds were part of the Waikiwi Domain off the end of Huia St. He soon became the Bowling Green Caretaker.

Percy and Elsie rest in St John's Cemetery, Waikiwi.

LILLIAN .... and CHURCH:

After their marriage Lillian and Nelson became members of the Presbyterian Church, corner Bourke and Windsor Streets, North Invercargill. Marlene and I attended Sunday School and the Church held Social Meetings where we learnt to dance.

On 15 July 1954 the Waverly Church Hall opened for Church Meetings. I was 17 and excused 'Church' if I washed our kitchen floor or made a steam pudding for Sunday lunch. I never washed the floor. On 7 December 1963 the new Waverly Church became operational. The book "A Venture Forward" printed in 1993 mentions Lillian on eight occasions .....
Page 29 .. 8 Sept 1954 records the first meeting of the Women's Fellowship, Lillian appointed to the committee. P31 .. Lillian on roster to clean the hall in August with Mrs Speirs. P48/49 photos of Lillian and others at 1957 Fellowship meeting and Nelson's mother Hannah joined by others of the Women's Missionary Union in 1957. P57 August 1962, Mrs L Price was appointed as representative of the Womens Fellowship to the Stewardship Committee. P66 1964, Lillian and other ladies volunteered to reduce the mortgage of the new Church by the Catering Group. Over 2 months they raised $652.00. P128/129 This photo shows Lillian and her fellow members of the New Church Executive.

NEW CHURCH EXECUTIVE AND ASSOCIATES, 1962
Back row: Rev. Robert Wilson (Chairman), Sid Radka, Eric Walker, Cliff Sneyd, Bob Liddell, Ted Collie
Front row: Bruce Burns, Lillian Price, Unah Borland, Margaret Harris, Herb Miles

P76 Lillian offered her phone number for people to order 200 Xmas trees in 1962.
P165 Mrs L Price still a member of the Catering Committee.

--oo00oo—

When Lillian died in January 1999 her family received this letter from Thelma Dermody of the Waverly Church leadership group.

"To Lillian's Family. We have never met, yet I feel I know you through your mother, speaking to me of you all, the grand and great grand children and the photos. I enjoyed Lillian's company and we had some good outings together and I feel privileged to have known her. On my last visit at home, she was speaking of her declining health, and being on her own, and we spoke about it. Lillian said 'I'm not afraid of death, I know where I am going, my only wish is I am never a burden to my family.' I thought you would wish to know she had said that. It was a comfort to me and I hope it will be to you. Lillian was very much admired among her friends. She never seemed in a rush, always immaculate and gracious and on time. A very well organised lady. I know she will be missed but you will have happy memories of holidays and family get togethers and these things no one can take away from you. Yours in sympathy, Thelma Dermody. "

--oo00oo—

PAGE 163 FAMILY BRIEF TREE

This shows Nelson & Lillian's 3 generations of direct ancestors and their 36 direct descendants, as at 1 September 2021.
Step-children noted *

For more information about Nelson's **Price** and Lillian's **Stevens** & **Thomas** families see "Morgan Price & family" 1991, "The Thomas family" 1993 and "The STEVENS family" 1999 books, available in some NZ Libraries.
Also refer ... www.tnprice.co.nz

NELSON PRICE and LILLIAN THOMAS ... BRIEF TREE

as at 1 September 2021

MORGAN PRICE b1808 m JANE THOMAS	**JOHN THOMAS** b1829 m JANE COATES
JOHN MORGAN PRICE b1835 m JANE McDONALD	**JOHN THOMAS** b1851 m PHEBE WOODS
JAMES McDONALD PRICE b1875 m HANNAH SOPER	**PERCIVAL WALTER THOMAS** b1881 m ELSIE STEVENS
NELSON PRICE married b1910 1935	**LILLIAN ELSIE THOMAS** b1912

3 children

10 Grandchildren
22 Gt Grandchildren
1 Gt Gt Grandchild

TREVOR PRICE	MARLENE PRICE	CHRISTOPHER PRICE
b1937 m JILL SOMERVILLE	b1939 m NOEL GORRIE	b1951 m ESTHER BRYAN
3 children	4 children	3 children

Jeffrey & Pauline	Tony & Kiri	Janene & Nick	Raewyn & Murray	Lianne & Per	Ritchie & Kim	Kyla & Peter	Matthew & Shelley	Jonathan & Kirsten	Hannah & Cheyne
Teresa	Zane	Emma	Kelly & Georgina	Lisa	Jessica	Hannah	Millie	Alaric*	Anasta
Melissa	Xanthe		Thomas	Christina		Samuel	Lizzie	Morgan*	Manaia
Kevin	Sean						Thomas	Hannah*	Thiago
Jason									Manaaki
									Jerome*
									Bailee*

PHOTOS OF LILLIAN IN VARIOUS CLOTHES and HATS and AT VARIOUS AGES.

This photo was copied from the Ashburton school photo below.

Lillian in top row, left corner.

School photo is dated ....
'1923 Standards 4 and 5' so, Lillian seems to be in the St 4 group and would be aged 11.

In her photo album this is headed ....

"JUST LEFT SCHOOL"

That would be the Invercargill, Southland Technical College, probably August to December aged 15 in 1927.

Another young photo of Lillian, probably in her late teens while living at the nursery in Invercargill.

Brother Hector, Lillian and Gordon the dog at Nursery.

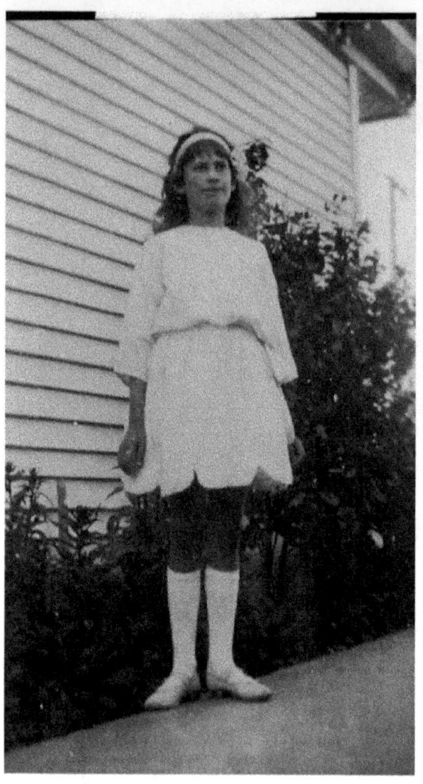

EARLY DAYS in INVERCARGILL

Lillian and her brothers .. Leslie at left and Hector.

Lillian & unknown lady

Above and below are Lillian and Jessie Hockings, and below with a friend.

Below is Jessie and her mother Daisy Hockings nee Stevens, and Lillian. Daisy was a sister of Lillian's mother Elsie Maud Thomas nee Stevens.

Above, the location and little girl unknown to me.

At the Ashton beach, below.

Lillian & Molly Macdonald

March 1937...
That is Trevor in the pram.

Top right Lillian at Thomas Bros Nursery, Waikiwi, Invercargill.

We have a **SKETCH BOOK** that Lillian did some drawing in. This work seems to have taken place during Lillian's early years at the Nursery when aged 17 and 18.

They are dated between April 1929 and July 1930.

The sketch book has one of these drawn to each page which measures 185 mm square and all are in pencil.
On the cover is written ... Lillian E Thomas. 1930.

LILLIAN'S SCRAP BOOK:

This is a very large book we have, with very little in it. Makes me wonder if there was an earlier one that maybe Chris has. The first pages contain newspaper articles of Lillian's Auckland Price grandchildren from about 1980. We include here some selections especially of those grandchildren who may not have got a mention in earlier parts of this book.

There are also a number of articles of her brother Hec Thomas, wife Ruby and their children, who lived in New Plymouth.

Granddaughter Janene Price (14) with friends Sarah Giblin and Katy Banks, travelling home from Takapuna Grammar, taken during a North Shore Council traffic survey about 1983.
(North Shore Times Advertiser)

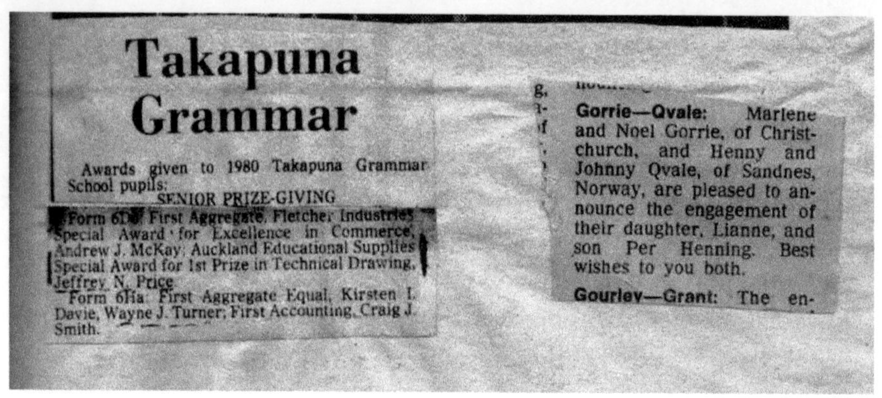

Takapuna Grammar

Awards given to 1980 Takapuna Grammar School pupils:

SENIOR PRIZE-GIVING

Form 6D: First Aggregate, Fletcher Industries Special Award for Excellence in Commerce, Andrew J. McKay; Auckland Educational Supplies Special Award for 1st Prize in Technical Drawing, Jeffrey N. Price.

Form 6Ha: First Aggregate Equal, Kirsten I. Davie, Wayne J. Turner; First Accounting, Craig J. Smith.

Gorrie—Qvale: Marlene and Noel Gorrie, of Christchurch, and Henny and Johnny Qvale, of Sandnes, Norway, are pleased to announce the engagement of their daughter, Lianne, and son Per Henning. Best wishes to you both.

Gourley—Grant: The en-

Grandson Jeffrey Price's 1980 prize, and
Granddaughter Lianne Gorrie's engagement notice to Per Qvale.

Christmas Cards from Lianne and Per to her grandmother contain photos of their children.

Upper ... Christmas 2007. CHRISTINA aged 13 and LISA 15 years.

Lower ... Christmas 1998. CHRISTINA aged 4 and LISA 6.5 years old.

This family lived in Norway.

21 April 1983 lead page of The North Shore Times Advertiser. This shows the staff welcoming the Winter Fashion Feature. Grandson Tony Price (lower right) worked there a while.

28 February 1995.
Photo from NZ Herald.

Granddaughter
Kyla Gorrie modelling a dress by "SOLO" at the Auckland Town Hall where nine of NZ's designers showed off their creations.

--oo00oo--

Below ....

Kyla Gorrie 12 May 1992, Network Administrator for Mayell Foods, maker of 'The Cookie Muncher', with workmate Melanie. (Christchurch Press)

NELSON & LILLIAN family INDEX:

INDEX for pages 120 - 182

THE FOLLOWING PAGES CAN BE USED TO RECORD NEW INFORMATION AND NEW BIRTHS, MARRIAGES AND DEATHS.

www.ingramcontent.com/pod-product-compliance
Ingram Content Group UK Ltd.
Pitfield, Milton Keynes, MK11 3LW, UK
UKHW020130250726
13967UKWH00002B/564

9 780473 600846